TS Iˢᵗ ENGLISH Part Viz ENGLISH EMPIRE containing yᵉ Articklands near Hudsons Bay New North & South Wales New Britain
olania or Florida California Sommer Iˢ Bahama Iˢ Jamaica &c. CARIBY Iˢ II SPANISH Pᵗ viz N Spain, of yᵉ Antilles III FRE
BAFFINS BAY
ARCTICK LAND
STRAITS
Hudsons Straits
NEW NORTH WALES
TERRA LABRADOR
HUDSONS BAY
NEW SOUTH WALES
NEW BRITAIN
James
NEW FOUND LAND
The Main Bank
False Bank
L PISCOUTAGAMY
L TABITIBIS
NEW FRANCE
LAKE SUPERIOR
LAKE HURONS
LAKE ILINOIS
LAKE ERIE
Land Wild Bulls
Cape Cod
THE ENGLISH EMPIRE
SEA OF THE ENGLISH EMPIRE
Bermudes als Summer Islands
THE GOLF OR BAY OF MEXICO
BAHAMA ISLANDS
C Florida
ANTILLES Iˢ
WEST INDIAN SEA
CARIBY ISLANDS
SOTTAVAN Iˢ
Tabasco
YUCATAN
HONDURAS
NEW ANDALUSIA

•VOICES• *from* COLONIAL AMERICA

CALIFORNIA

1542–1850

ROBIN DOAK

WITH

ANDRÉS RESÉNDEZ, PH.D., CONSULTANT

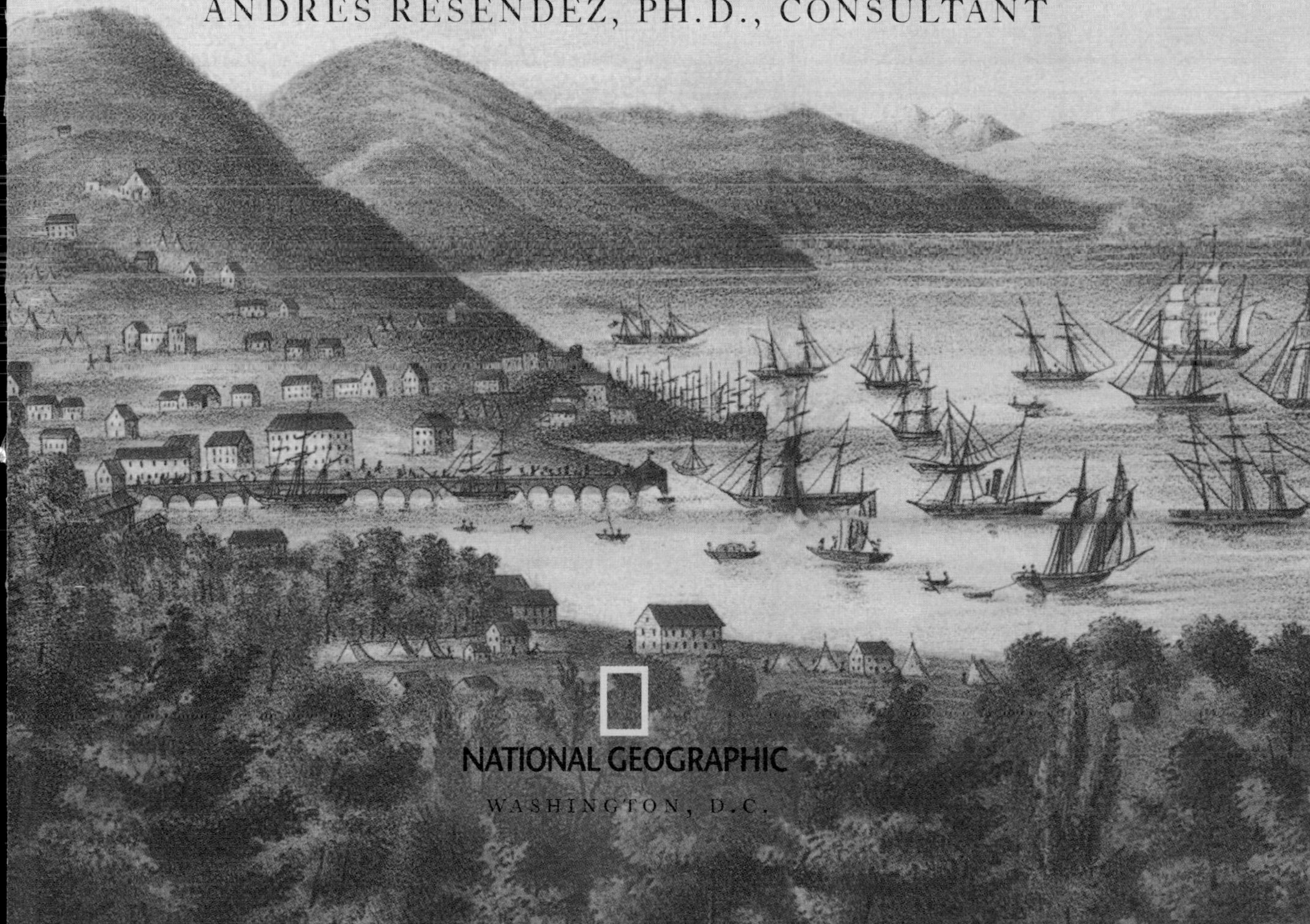

NATIONAL GEOGRAPHIC
WASHINGTON, D.C.

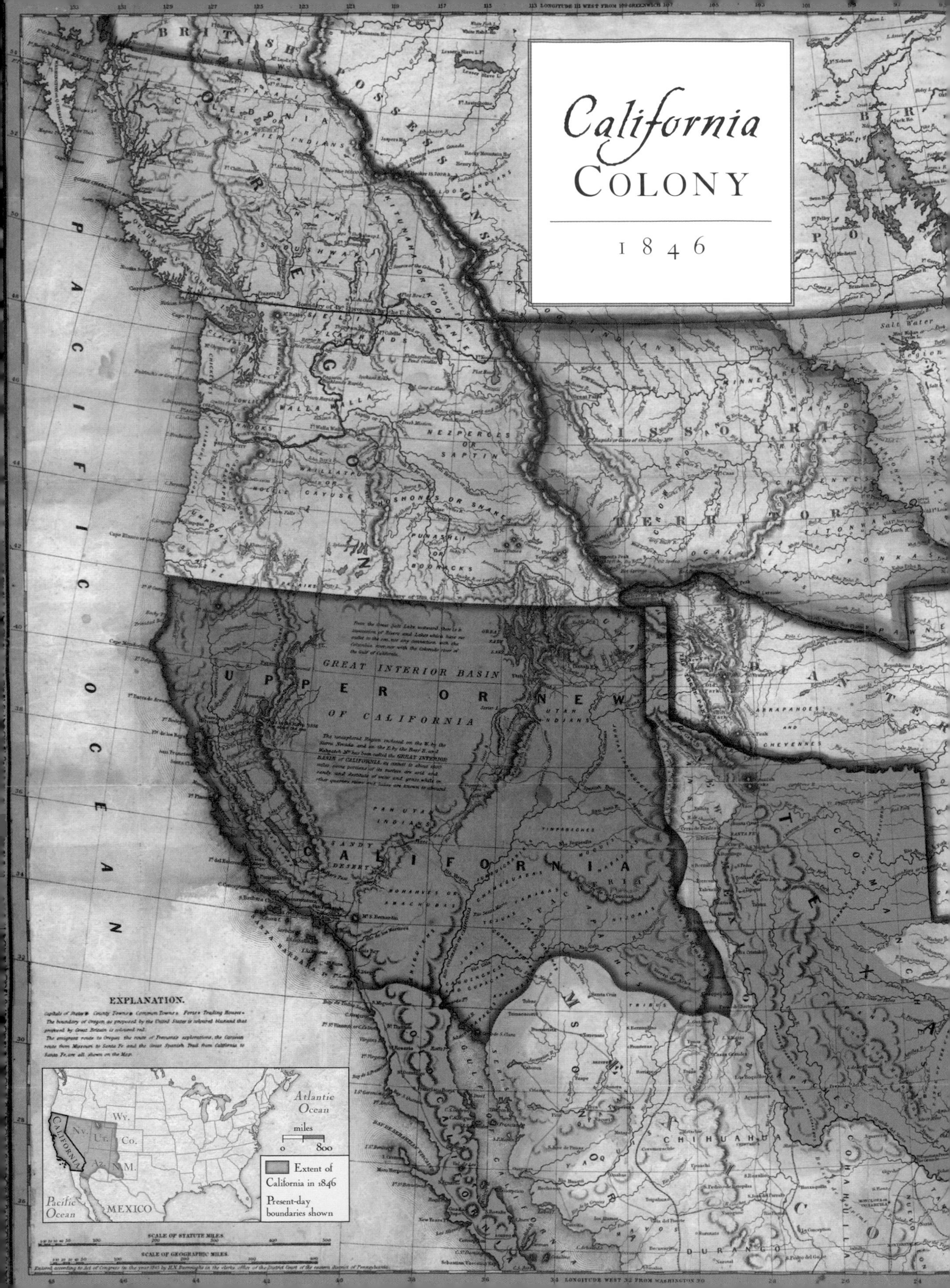
California
COLONY
1846
BRITISH POSSESSIONS
PACIFIC OCEAN
OREGON
MISSOURI TERRITORY
GREAT INTERIOR BASIN
UPPER OR NEW
OF CALIFORNIA
CALIFORNIA
NEW MEXICO
CHIHUAHUA
DURANGO
EXPLANATION.
Capitals of States County Towns Common Towns Forts Trading Houses
The boundary of Oregon as proposed by the United States is coloured blue and that proposed by Great Britain is coloured red.
The emigrant route to Oregon the route of Fremont's explorations, the Caravan route from Missouri to Santa Fe and the Great Spanish Trail from California to Santa Fe are all shown on the Map.
Atlantic Ocean
Wy.
Nv.
Ut.
Co.
Az.
N.M.
CALIFORNIA
Pacific Ocean
MEXICO
miles
0
800
Extent of California in 1846
Present-day boundaries shown
SCALE OF STATUTE MILES
SCALE OF GEOGRAPHIC MILES

INTRODUCTION

by

Andrés Reséndez, Ph.D.

Native Americans of California belong to the Pomo, Chumash, Mojave, and Shoshone tribes, among others. Five Indians in traditional dress, some with tattoos on their faces, are shown in this hand-colored lithograph

The state of California has reinvented itself many times over. With every reinvention its past seems more distant. Hollywood, Disneyland, and the high-tech communities of Silicon Valley speak of a new place, a place always looking to the future. The traffic jams in Los Angeles, the modernist architecture of San Diego,

OPPOSITE: This map, published in 1846 in Philadelphia, shows the Mexican territory of Upper California in red. The inset map labels present-day California as well as other states with land that was included in this region for comparison.

even the large agribusinesses of the Central Valley are all products of the 20th century. Yet, if we go beyond mere appearances we'll find many signs of California's deep roots in the past.

For all of California's current glitz and global reach, its colonial beginnings were remarkably modest. When Europeans first reached the area that we call the Golden State, they found an extraordinary variety of native peoples (by the sheer number of languages spoken, it was one of the most diverse regions anywhere on the planet). Such diversity, although remarkable, was hardly favorable to the European powers looking to expand their empires through colonization. Before the Spanish missionaries, soldiers, and settlers found their way to California and built a string of missions, presidios, and a few pueblos, there was little interest in the region.

To explore this history is to venture into a world of diverse native groups well adapted to California's environment. For instance, many of these societies of hunters and gatherers relied heavily on acorns, giving rise to a very productive type of agricultural system that is seldom found anywhere else. At the same time, it is a story of determined European pioneers. California was rather distant from Mexico City, the capital of New Spain, and a world apart from other centers of Spanish power such as the cities of Seville or Madrid. Conditions were rugged and simple at best. Friars and soldiers had to labor very hard in California to eke out a living while attempting to convert the natives to Christianity and ultimately "civilize" them. According to the Spanish, this was a project that had both positive and negative consequences.

Finally, California is a story of rapid and profound transformation. Under Mexican rule, the colony developed a prosperous ranching and commercial economy. In turn, this social and economic order was overwhelmed by immigrants from many corners of North America and the world with the discovery of gold. This volume will introduce young readers to California's rich past and help them understand how an outpost of empire became an empire in itself.

AN ACCOUNT OF
CALIFORNIA,
AND THE
WONDERFUL GOLD REGIONS.
A New Arrival at the Gold Diggings.
WITH A DESCRIPTION OF
The Different Routes to California;
Information about the Country, and the Ancient and Modern Discoveries of Gold;
How to Test Precious Metals; Accounts of Gold Hunters;
TOGETHER WITH MUCH OTHER
Useful Reading for those going to California, or having Friends there.
ILLUSTRATED WITH MAPS AND ENGRAVINGS.
BOSTON:
PUBLISHED BY J. B. HALL, 66 CORNHILL.
For Sale at Skinner's Publication Rooms, 60½ Cornhill.
Price, 12½ cents.

This pamphlet, printed and distributed in Boston, Massachusetts, in 1849, directed immigrants to the goldfields of California. Advertisements like this fueled the mass migration to northern California that came to be known as the gold rush.

C H A P T E R   O N E

Early Explorers

Spanish and English explorers *claim California for their countries, but the region remains unsettled by Europeans.*

The history of colonial California begins in the mid-1500s, when Spanish explorers began scouting the region. Despite early explorations, however, the Spaniards chose to neglect California and focus their energies on other parts of New Spain. New Spain was the name for all Spain's possessions in the New World north of Panama. Spanish territory in North America included Mexico and the southern part of what is now the United States. The capital of New Spain was Mexico City.

OPPOSITE: In 1579, Sir Francis Drake, sailing for England, was greeted by friendly Native Americans who lived along the northern California coast. This illustration shows a local tribe placing a feathered crown on Drake's head and performing a ritual dance in his honor.

Spain began its conquest of the New World in 1492, when explorer Christopher Columbus claimed several Caribbean islands for the country. In the coming years, Spanish conquistadores took control of Mexico, then branched out from there.

conquistadores—Spanish soldiers who defeated the Indians of Mexico and other places in the Americas

In the mid-1530s, conquistador Hernán Cortés discovered the peninsula that is known today as Baja (Lower) California. The Spanish, believing their new discovery was an island, named the region for an imaginary island called California. This invented island, featured in a Spanish book written in 1510, was said to be a paradise, home to a tribe of female warriors called Amazons. Cortés was just one of many Spaniards who believed that such a paradise actually existed. He had been told by Indians in Mexico that an island, *"completely populated by women, with no men among them,"* lay to the north.

Alta California

In 1542, Portuguese explorer Juan Rodríguez Cabrillo became the first European to explore the coast of present-day California. Like other Spanish explorers of the time, Cabrillo hoped to find a passage between the North Pacific and North Atlantic Oceans. (In 1854, this pathway through the icy waters of the Arctic, the Northwest Passage, was finally discovered.)

The Island of CALIFORNIA

In 1539, Spanish explorer Francisco de Ulloa was the first to learn that Baja California was not an island. Sailing from Acapulco, Ulloa traveled up the western coast of Mexico, then down the eastern coast of Baja California, proving that the two were connected by land. The news was not widely reported, however, and it would not be until 1705 that a map was created that showed California connected to the rest of North America. The map was drawn by Spanish explorer and missionary Eusebio Kino. By the 1750s, most maps showed Baja California correctly.

Cabrillo didn't discover the Strait of Anián (the Spanish name for the Northwest Passage), but on September 28, he became the first European to enter present-day San Diego Bay. Cabrillo claimed the entire region for Spain, naming it Alta (Upper) California. He named the bay San Miguel Arcángel.

During the visit, Cabrillo and his men met some of the Native Americans in the area, including the Chumash. At first, the Indians *"gave signs of great fear."* Three men approached the Spaniards and, using sign language, related that people who were *"bearded, clothed, and armed"* like the newcomers had been killing natives to the west. Historians believe that these bearded men were probably part of a Spanish expedition of conquest heading through present-day New Mexico and Arizona. The reactions of other tribes that

Cabrillo met were mixed. Although some Indians welcomed the newcomers, others shot arrows at them and fled.

After resting at San Diego, Cabrillo and his men sailed north, traveling as far as present-day San Francisco. Along the way, the ships stopped to visit Native American villages, hoping to obtain information that would lead them to their goal. After sailing north, the group turned around and headed south, hoping to find a safe place to spend the winter months. At some point, Cabrillo fell and broke his arm. Gangrene set in, and in January 1543, the explorer died off the coast of Santa Barbara. He was buried on an island. Cabrillo's men resumed sailing north, possibly reaching as far as the present-day border of California and Oregon.

gangrene—the death and decay of tissues in the body

Native Californians

During his voyage, Cabrillo met Native Americans who were descended from Asians who had migrated across the Bering Strait to Alaska more than 11,000 years ago. These early people continued south, settling throughout present-day California.

At the time of European contact, historians believe that California was the most densely populated region north of Mexico. The area was home to as many as 275,000 people, members of dozens of tribes. These tribes included the Pomo, Chumash, Mojave, Karok, Yuma, Paiute, and Shoshone.

Native Americans of the San Francisco Bay area hunted small game to add to their diets of nuts, berries, and fish.

The tribes of California became very different from each other over the years. These differences were the result of living in many different regions in California—coastline, mountains, valleys, deserts, and forests. As time went on, tribes isolated from one another by mountains and deserts developed their own languages and customs.

Nearly all the California tribes were hunter-gatherers. They relied on nuts, berries, fish, and game for their food. The most important food was acorns from oak trees. Because of the importance of the acorn, each tribe cared for its own grove of oak trees. Each fall, the trees were shaken, and the women collected the fallen acorns. The nuts were then stored in large baskets that hung from poles. Acorn meat had to be specially prepared before it could be eaten.

First, a bitter substance called tannic acid had to be removed. To do this, native women ground the acorn meat into flour on a flat stone. The flour was then rinsed several times with hot water. Acorn flour was most often mixed with water and cooked in baskets to make a thick soup. The Chumash ate this porridge-like substance with nearly every meal.

tannic acid—a bitter acid found in plants

The Chumash, who lived along the coast between present-day San Luis Obispo and Los Angeles, were also known for their fishing skills. They built tomol, large wooden canoes measuring from 8 to 30 feet (2.4 to 9 m). Tribes throughout California supplemented their diets by hunting deer and smaller animals. In the dry and arid Great Basin region, people caught and ate grasshoppers.

Two tribes in California, the Yuma and the Mojave, grew their own crops. These two groups lived in the fertile regions along the Colorado River, which forms the southeast border of the present-day state. The tribes grew corn, beans, squash, and pumpkins.

Most California tribes lived in villages of 100 to 500 people. When the Spanish arrived, they called these villages rancherias. The homes of Chumash and other tribes were simple, made with willow and other tree branches that stood upright and were bent at the top to form a dome. More branches were then tied horizontally around the structure to form a frame. Finally, these

rancheria— Spanish name for a Native American village; later, a ranch where Indians lived and worked near the missions

branches were covered with rushes and cattails. A hole at the top of the home allowed air in and smoke from a cooking fire out. This hole could easily be covered with animal skins when it rained. The size of the houses varied. Missionary Juan Crespí wrote, *"without a doubt seventy persons could enter."*

Chumash and many other tribal villages also had a sweat house. The sweat house was the way that native Californians kept clean. Sweat houses came in all sizes, with large ones built partially below ground. A ladder in the roof of a big sweat house allowed tribal members, usually men, access. (Women sometimes used the sweat house for religious or healing ceremonies.) The room, warmed by pouring water on rocks heating in a fire pit to create steam, served as a place for the men to socialize. After sweating for a while, the men would scrape their skin with a piece of wood, then go outside and jump in a creek to cool off.

A sweat house, used by the Chumash to clean themselves, was also a place where men gathered to socialize. One member of the tribe (right) tends the fire where rocks are heated. In the foreground, another tribe member lifts the flap of the sweat house to enter.

Most California tribes had very little political structure. The chief was the head of the tribe. However, chiefs often had little real authority. The real leader of the tribe was the shaman, also called a medicine man (though a shaman could be a man or a woman). The shaman performed ceremonies to heal sickness and pain.

shaman—a Native American healer or medicine man

The Sea Dog Arrives

In June 1579, English sea captain Sir Francis Drake arrived off the California coast. Although the exact location of Drake's landfall is unknown, it was probably somewhere near San Francisco. Drake was a "sea dog," a pirate authorized by Queen Elizabeth I of England to attack Spanish ships.

Drake had just finished raiding Spanish settlements and capturing Spanish trading ships along the coast of South and Central America. Now, he and his men spent five weeks relaxing in California. Like Cabrillo before him, Drake visited several Native American groups in the region. Before he set sail for home across the Pacific Ocean, he left behind a brass marker, naming the area Nova Albion (New England) and claiming it for England.

Drake's visit sparked renewed Spanish interest in the California coast. The Spanish didn't want England to jeopardize their valuable trade with China. Just a few years before Drake's arrival, the Spanish had pioneered a trading route from Acapulco in Mexico to Manila in the Philippines. Manila, settled by the Spanish in 1571, had become a trading center, where silver from Mexico was traded for spices and other goods from China. On the return trip from

Manila, Spanish ships were carried by strong ocean currents to the coast of California. From there, they sailed south, back home to Acapulco.

In 1602 Spanish merchant, Sebastián Vizcaíno was hired to map the coastline and to find a good location for a port to supply Spanish ships sailing from Manila to Acapulco. He took six months and five days to sail from Acapulco to present-day San Diego. Along the way, Vizcaíno named many places in California, including San Diego, Santa Barbara, and Monterey.

SCURVY

VIZCAÍNO'S LONG SEA VOYAGE to California came at a high cost. By the time he reached the area, most of his men were suffering from scurvy. Scurvy is a disease caused by lack of vitamin C in the diet. As a result of their sickness, the sailors couldn't stop along California's coast. They were able to drop anchor, but unless they spent a long time on land recovering, they were too weak to pull the heavy anchor back up.

Vizcaíno returned to Mexico with high praise for California. However, the viceroy who had sent the merchant on his mission was replaced shortly after Vizcaíno returned home. The new viceroy had no interest in creating a port in California, and in 1606, a royal order prohibited further exploration of the region. Spanish settlement there was once again put on hold.

viceroy—a Spanish official in New Spain, similar to a governor

CHAPTER TWO

Protecting Spanish Interests

1765 – 1776

SPANISH SOLDIERS *and missionaries from New Spain found the first settlements in California.*

or more than 160 years, no Spanish ships explored California's coast. Then, in 1765, an unexpected event brought the Spanish back to California: Russian traders from Alaska, more than 2,300 miles (3,700 km) away, appeared off the coast of San Francisco.

OPPOSITE: In the rich coastal waters off northern California, an Aleut Indian hunts fur seals for pelts to trade with the Russians, whose ship is in the inlet beyond. The number of seals soon declined, however, due to overhunting, and the Aleuts returned to Alaska.

The Russians had first gone to Alaska in 1741, when explorer Vitus Bering landed there. Although Bering died on the way back to Russia, some of his crew made it home. They told stories of a land rich in fur-bearing animals. Russian traders and trappers soon returned to Alaska and set up trading posts. The Russians traded for furs with the Aleuts, Native Americans from the Aleutian Islands in Alaska, and hired them to hunt seals and sea otters. In search of furs, the Russians and Aleutians together moved farther and farther south down the west coast of North America until, in 1765, they reached islands off the coast of present-day San Francisco.

The Spanish Stake a Claim

Reports of the Russian presence off the coast of San Francisco trickled back to Mexico City. Worried that the Russians intended to establish a colony there, the Spanish decided that the time had come to settle California. A Spanish settlement in the region would also discourage Spain's enemy, Great Britain, from asserting Sir Francis Drake's claim to the region.

New Spain's visitador-general, or inspector general, José de Gálvez, was the mastermind of the plan to colonize the San Diego and Monterey Bay areas. Gálvez planned and found funding for the

visitador-general—a colonial official in New Spain

expedition. He even built a port at San Blas on the west coast of Mexico to serve as a supply post for the future settlements in California.

PROFILE

José de Gálvez

José de Gálvez was born in Málaga, Spain, in 1720. A successful attorney and judge, Gálvez was appointed visitador-general of New Spain in 1765. Although politically powerful, the new official suffered from bouts of serious mental illness. At one time, Gálvez considered importing 600 monkeys from Guatemala, dressing them in soldiers' uniforms, and training them to fight against rebellious natives. Anyone who dared accuse him of insanity, however, was promptly thrown into prison. Despite problems with his mental health, Gálvez was a tireless advocate for the settlement of California. He spent six years in New Spain before being appointed Minister of the Indies.

The plan to colonize California, called the "Sacred Expedition," began in early 1769. The expedition consisted of two groups that traveled by land and two small ships carrying additional soldiers, missionaries, livestock, and supplies. A third ship filled with supplies, the *San José*, would be sent later.

The expedition was headed by Gaspar de Portolá, the first governor of Baja California. In 1697, Jesuit missionaries had been given permission to colonize that part of New Spain. The Jesuits were members of a Roman Catholic religious order, the Society of Jesus. In 1767, however, Spain's King Carlos III expelled the Jesuits from the region and put Portolá in charge of Baja California. Now Portolá's goal was to protect Spain's interest in the region by building presidios and missions at present-day San Diego and Monterey.

presidio—a Spanish fort or military post

mission—in California, a settlement founded by the Franciscans for the purpose of converting Native Americans to Christianity

The first ship, the *San Carlos*, set sail from La Paz, in Baja California, in January 1769, followed by the *San Antonio* a month later. In March, the first of the overland parties headed north under the command of Captain Fernando de Rivera y Moncada. The last part of the expedition left in May. This overland group was commanded by Portolá himself, accompanied by Father Junípero Serra. Serra, a Franciscan missionary, was the head of all the Catholic missions in Baja California.

Franciscan—a member of a Roman Catholic order founded by Saint Francis

Whether traveling by sea or by land, the members of the expedition had a difficult journey. The *San Antonio* arrived in San Diego after 55 days, but the *San Carlos* took twice as long. By the time the two ships reached their destination, 24 men had died from scurvy and the rest were sick with the disease.

Gaspar de Portolá's overland party that explored San Diego in 1769 included Father Junípero Serra (standing in gray robe), who later founded Mission San Diego de Alcalá.

Men traveling overland had to cross mountains and deserts and were attacked by groups of hostile Indians. By July 1, all four groups had arrived in San Diego. The supply ship *San José,* sent after the first two ships, never arrived. Of the 219 men who had left Baja California, fewer than 100 survived the journey.

With all the men finally together, Portolá chose the healthiest and set off north in search of Monterey. During this leg of the expedition, the group experienced the first earthquake ever recorded in California's history. While camped about 30 miles (48 km) southeast of present-day Los Angeles, the party felt several strong tremors. Father Juan Crespí recorded that two of the quakes lasted for *"less than a Hail Mary."* In recent years, seismologists have performed tests that indicate that the 1769 quake was a major one, perhaps the largest in Los Angeles history.

seismologist—a scientist who studies

As Portolá's expedition continued north toward Monterey, they met many Native Americans. Like Vizcaíno before him, Portolá found that while some tribes were friendly, others were afraid of the Spanish explorers. Father Crespí reported,

> *When they came to explore this place, at the same spot where we are stopping the scouts found a very big heathen (unconverted) village that they said must have amounted to over 500 souls, so exceedingly ill-behaved that it cost them a great deal of trouble to pacify them and give them to understand we were coming in peace and not in order to harm them. They did make peace, laying down all their weapons, but the fact is that we arrived [after the scouts] and found burnt and abandoned the village where they had been, and not a heathen to be seen anywhere here.*

Years later, Pablo Tac, an Indian who had spent most of his life at Mission San Luis Rey, recorded how one tribe viewed the new arrivals:

> *When the missionary arrived in our country with a small troop, our captain and also the others were astonished. . . . But when they drew near, then the captain got up . . . and met them. They halted and the missionary then began to speak, the captain saying perhaps in his language . . . "What is it that you seek here? Get out of our country!" But they did not understand him, and they answered him in Spanish, and the captain began with signs, and the Fernandino [missionary], understanding him, gave him gifts and in this manner made him his friend.*

The First Spanish Settlements

On July 16, Serra founded Mission San Diego de Alcalá. The mission, which was part of a presidio, was the first in what would become a 530-mile (853-km)–long string of 21 Spanish missions, stretching from San Diego to Sonoma. Mission San Diego had humble beginnings. It consisted of a few huts made of sticks and mud. In 1774, the mission would be moved away from the presidio and closer to a nearby Indian village.

Over the next 60 years, area natives would be forced to give up their lifestyles and accept a European way of living. The mission period also saw a drastic drop in California's Indian population. When the first mission was founded, California was home to as many as 300,000 American Indians. By the time the United States took control of California in 1848, that number had been reduced to about 100,000. Diseases introduced during the mission period took a deadly toll on the local tribes.

Failing to find Monterey, Portolá returned to San Diego in late January 1770. There, he found the men in rough shape.

After the arrival of a supply ship, Portolá again set out to find Monterey. This time, he succeeded. A presidio and mission, Mission San Carlos Borromeo de Monterey, were founded on June 3. Monterey would serve as the first capital of California.

Connecting the Colonies

By late 1772, Franciscan missionaries had founded three more missions in California. Officials in New Spain realized that they needed a good route to their northern colony. In early 1774, Juan Bautista de Anza set out to explore and map that route. Anza began his expedition in Tubac, the first Spanish settlement in Arizona, just north of Mexico, which had been founded in 1752. From Tubac, Anza and his party followed the Gila River to the Colorado River, then continued to Mission San Diego. Anza returned to Tubac in May 1774.

In early 1775, Anza set out on a second overland trip to California. In January 1776, Anza and his party arrived at Mission San Gabriel, built in 1771 near the San Gabriel River. Two months later, they arrived at the presidio at Monterey. Soon after arriving, Anza traveled to San Francisco Bay and selected a site for the future presidio and mission of San Francisco de Asís.

In June 1776, the settlers from Monterey moved to San Francisco and began building the presidio and mission there. On the other side of North America, the soon-to-be-signed Declaration of Independence would result in years of bloody warfare between Britain and its rebellious colonies. At the end of the American Revolution in 1783, a new country, the United States of America, would be born. Although no one knew it at the time, this new nation would have a profound effect on the future of California. ⁂

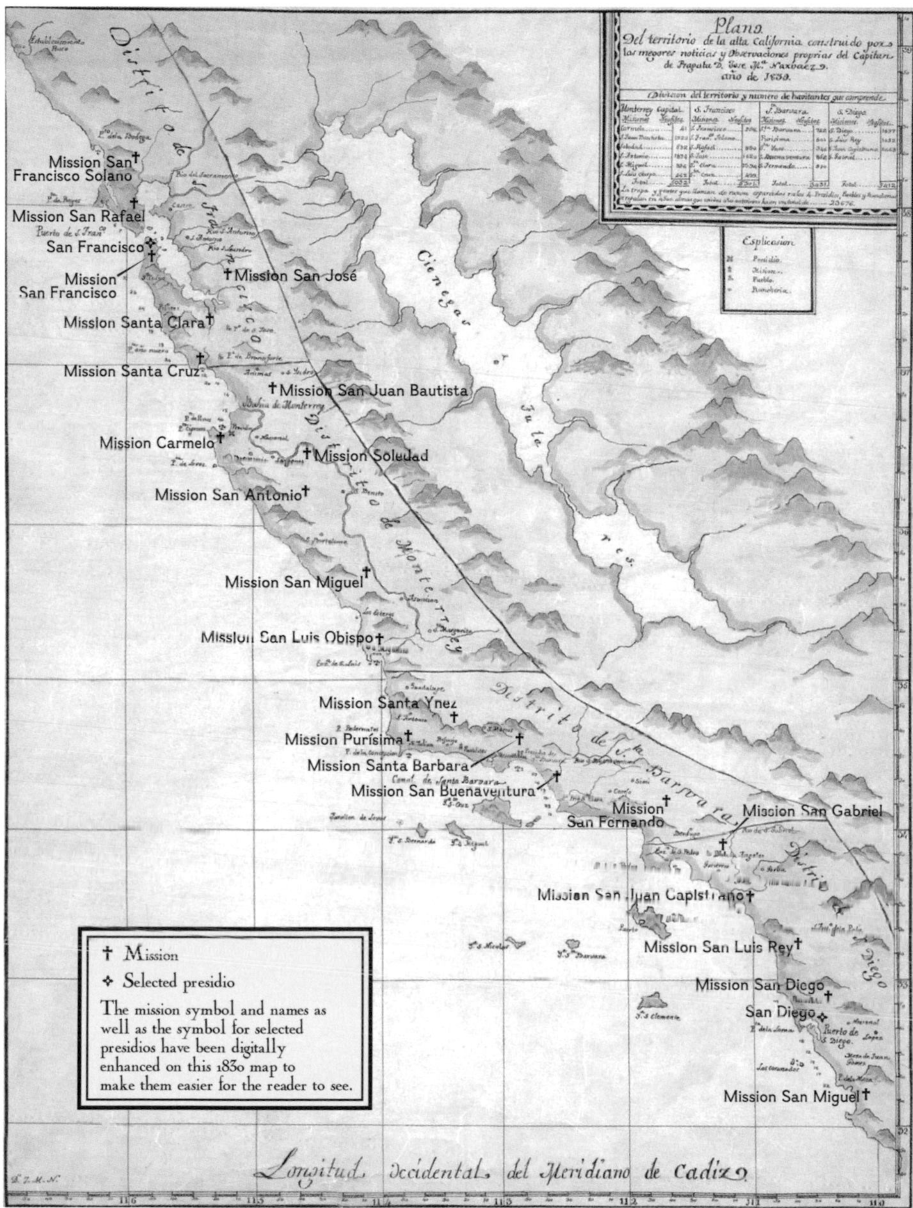

This map, drawn by José María Narváez, shows the missions, presidios, pueblos, and rancherias (ranches) that existed in four coastal districts (marked by the red lines)—San Franciso, Monterey, Santa Barbara, and San Diego—of Mexican California in 1830. To highlight the missions, which stretched from San Diego in the south to Sonoma in the north, the symbol and names have been enhanced for the reader. According to the key on Narváez's map, missions in San Diego had 5,412 neophytes, more than any other district.

Life at the Missions

Mission life in *colonial California is difficult— especially for the thousands of natives who are forced to convert to Christianity.*

alifornia's first European settlers were Franciscan missionaries. These men, many from Spain, volunteered to come to New Spain and spend ten years preaching to the Native Americans. Before the founding of Mission San Diego in 1769, Spanish missions already existed in present-day Florida, Texas, New Mexico, and Arizona.

The chief goal of the mission was to convert the Native Americans to Christianity. Another goal was to "civilize"

OPPOSITE: A view of Mission San Diego de Alcalá shows the church (right) and other buildings that probably provided storage for food, a laundry, and shelter for the friars and converted natives.

them, or, in the words of English visitor Frederick William Beechey, to "*train them up within the walls of the establishment in the exercise of a good life, and of some trade, so that they may in time be able to provide for themselves and become useful members of civilised society.*" For the Indians, becoming civilized meant adopting new ways of working, living, eating, and speaking.

Attracting Converts

Mission San Diego de Alcalá had a rocky start. At first, the Native Americans did not welcome the newcomers. Soon after the Franciscan missionaries arrived at San Diego, they were attacked by Indians. Soldiers at the mission fired their guns to drive them away, but hostilities continued, and during the first year of the mission's existence, the missionaries were unable to convert any Indians. Despite this failure and many hardships—including severe hunger, an inadequate water supply, and the threat of Indian attacks—the Franciscans remained in San Diego.

Eventually, the missions were able to convert some of the Native Americans to Christianity. There are no data on how many natives willingly chose to convert and how many were forcibly captured by Spanish soldiers and taken to the missions. The strategy for some missionaries was to capture children and women, because parents, spouses, and other relatives would soon follow their loved ones into the missions. One neophyte

neophyte—a Native American who had been baptized by the missionaries at Mission Santa Cruz described how children were taken: *"The padres would erect a hut and light the candles to say mass and the Indians, attracted by the lights—thinking they were stars—would approach, and soon be taken."*

Spanish missionaries preach to an assembled group of Native Americans, some already converted, in California.

Other Indians came willingly, attracted by gifts of beads or food. Once the Indians were securely inside mission walls, they were baptized and began their new life as neophytes, as the missionaries called them. (Natives who were not converted were called gentiles.) Beechey described the way many Indians came to be baptized:

> *. . . if any of the captured Indians show a repugnance to conversion, it is the practice to imprison them for a few days and then to allow them to breathe a little fresh air in a walk round the mission, to observe the happy mode of life of their converted countrymen; after which they are again shut up, until they declare their readiness to renounce the religion of their forefathers.*

During the mission period, from 1769 to roughly 1829, Franciscan missionaries converted nearly 17,000 California Indians to Christianity and a European culture.

PROFILE

Father Junípero Serra

California's most famous missionary, Father Junípero Serra, was born Miguel Juan Serra on the island of Majorca, Spain, in 1713. Serra became a Franciscan when he was 18.

In 1749, Serra volunteered to become a missionary in New Spain. He spent his first 17 years in the New World in north-central Mexico. There he gained followers by acting out the punishments suffered by the saints.

In 1769, Serra took part in the Portolá expedition to establish California's first missions. He spent the rest of his life in California, founding nine missions and baptizing as many as 6,000 Native Americans. Although Serra often tried to protect the Indians from the harsh treatment of the Spanish soldiers, he also favored physically punishing the neophytes when they did not follow the mission's rules. Serra's personal qualities of fairness and piety, however, attracted many Indians to Christianity.

Although his desire was to die a martyr for the Roman Catholic Church, the 70-year-old missionary died peacefully in Monterey in 1784. He is buried at the mission there.

Life of a Neophyte

Once baptized, the neophytes were kept within the mission itself or on a ranchería near the mission. At the mission, unmarried men and women were separated from each other. Women and children were housed in the main mission building, where the missionaries kept them under lock and key. Outside the mission fence, married neophytes and their families lived at the ranchería in thatched huts or adobe houses.

adobe—bricks made of clay

To make sure that the neophytes didn't wander away, each mission was home to four or five soldiers. These resident watchdogs lived at the mission's guardhouse. The entire mission compound, including the rancherías, was enclosed by a palisade fence or wall.

Every minute of the day, the neophytes were under the strict supervision of the missionaries. The days were structured, with time set aside for study, prayer, and labor. Bells at the mission called the community to work, prayer, and meals. One missionary described the importance of the bells, noting that the Indians "*are ignorant of the calendar. Though their language has distinct words for morning, noon, evening and night, the pagans [unconverted Indians] live to suit their fancy, do not understand anything about this as far as eating, working and resting [are] concerned. The neophytes are guided in every thing by the Mission Bell.*"

Because the main goal of the missionaries was to convert the Indians to Catholicism, prayer was an important part of each day, and neophytes had to attend church services each morning. In 1826, Beechey described a mass with the soldiers roaming the aisles *"with whips, canes, and goads to preserve silence and maintain order, and what seemed more difficult than either, to keep the congregation in their kneeling posture. The goads . . . would reach a long way and inflict a sharp puncture without making any noise. The end of the church was occupied by a guard of soldiers under arms with fixed bayonets."*

goad—a sharp, pointed stick usually used to herd cattle

At the Pala Mission, named for the small Pala tribe that lived along the San Luis Rey River in southern California, converted Indians attend a mass. The priest in the background of the drawing is wearing a costume adorned with skull and crossbones, signifying that this is a mass for the dead.

At many missions, the living conditions for neophytes were uncomfortable and dirty. The small, cramped huts were unsanitary and, therefore, unhealthy. As a result, disease was common, and most missions had a high death rate. Between 1806 and 1810, for example, a measles epidemic killed more than one-third of the neophytes at the five San Francisco-area missions. Many neophytes also suffered from malnutrition. They were not used to a steady diet of cornmeal and oatmeal, and many had trouble digesting the food.

Children were especially at risk from these diseases. According to one estimate, as many as half of all neophyte children died before reaching the age of four.

Making the Missions Work

Without Indian labor, the missions would have failed. Because of the difficulty in getting supplies from New Spain, each mission had to quickly become self-sustaining. In the early days of each mission, the newly converted neophytes provided the physical strength to build the mission churches, homes, and other structures.

The neophytes also kept the missions running by taking care of its day-to-day needs. One important activity was ranching. Each mission kept cattle and sheep. Indian vaqueros tended the cattle, rounded them up, and slaughtered them. The meat was eaten by mission residents, and the hides were traded for

vaquero—a cowboy

other goods. The sheep provided the wool needed for clothing and blankets made by neophyte women. By 1832, ranching had become the most important mission industry. There were more than 150,000 cattle on California missions.

Neophytes also tended the mission gardens and crops that supplied food for the missions and nearby presidios and pueblos. The food grown on some missions also supplied the Spanish trading ships that stopped in California on their way back to Mexico from Manila, in the Philippines. The neophytes learned to grow and harvest wheat, barley, corn, beans, and peas. In the orchards, they picked pears and apples. Men might also be taught a trade. Some neophytes became millers, carpenters, blacksmiths, and cobblers.

Neophyte women were not allowed to be idle, either. They were taught to wash, comb, straighten, and then weave sheep's wool into clothing, blankets, and

El Camino Real

El Camino Real, or the Royal Highway, was the route that connected the 21 California missions to each other. From San Diego in the south to Sonoma in the north, it stretched for about 530 miles (965 km). Each mission was located about a day's ride on horseback from the next. El Camino Real, the chief road in the colony, allowed travelers to move easily from one end of California to the other.

Today, the Royal Highway is covered over by modern roadways. Replicas of mission bells on the roadsides mark the old pathway.

rugs. They also learned how to sew. They cooked, cleaned, and performed other domestic chores for the missionaries.

Mission PETS

THE MISSIONARIES BROUGHT the first cats and dogs to California both as pets and, in the case of cats, as helpers. The cats kept down the rodent population. Father Font wrote of the new feline arrivals, *"They are very welcome . . . on account of the great abundance of mice."*

THE MISSIONARIES

During the six decades of the mission era, 142 Franciscan missionaries volunteered their time and effort to convert the Indians in California. (Fifty-eight of the missionaries died there.) All had one thing in common: They saw the Native Americans as savages who needed to be saved. In 1776, Father Pedro Font wrote, "*I might inquire what sin was committed by these Indians and their ancestors that they should grow up in these remote lands of the north with such infelicity and unhappiness, in such nakedness and misery, and above all, with such blind ignorance of everything.*"

The success of a mission often depended upon who was in charge. Mission San Luis Rey was headed by Father Antonio Peyri. Founded in 1798, San Luis Rey was the 18th mission. Because of Father Peyri's kind treatment of the Indians in the region, the mission soon had hundreds of neophytes. By 1825, there were more than 2,800 new converts, the largest neophyte population in an American mission. Father Peyri truly loved his mission. After he left California to return to Spain, he admitted, "*I confess that I have been very much disappointed in having left my California in order to come to my country.*"

Not all of the missionaries were as fond of California as Father Peyri. One wrote,

> *There are difficulties all around and I am overburdened with cares which render life wearisome. There is hardly anything of the religious in me, and I scarcely know what to do in these troubling times. I made the vows of a [Franciscan]; instead, I must manage the Indians, sow grain, raise sheep, horses and cows. I must preach, baptize, bury the dead, visit the sick, direct the carts, haul stones, lime etc. These are things incompatible, thorny, bitter, hard and unbearable. They rob me of time, tranquility and my health. I desire with lively anxiety to devote myself to my sacred ministry and to serve the Lord.*"

Other missionaries quickly became frustrated by—and intolerant of—California's native people. "*The Indians of California may be compared to a species of monkey,*" wrote Father Geronimo Boscana, "*for naught do they express interest, except in imitating the actions of others. . . . The Indian in his grave, humble and retired manner, conceals a hypocritical and treacherous disposition.*"

Such harsh views often led to cruel treatment of the neophytes. In 1799, Padre Antonio de la Concepción Horra of Mission San Miguel reported to New Spain's viceroy, "*The treatment shown to the Indians is the most cruel I have ever read in history. For the slightest things, they receive heavy flogging, are shackled, and put in stocks, and treated with so much cruelty that they are kept whole days without water.*" Padre Antonio was promptly declared insane and escorted from California to Mexico by Spanish soldiers.

In this view of the presidio at Monterey, California, neophytes tend to the fields, Indian women hang laundry, and a friar sits on horseback, overseeing the Indians' work. Sailing ships in the harbor probably brought needed supplies to the mission.

RESISTING THE MISSIONARIES

The neophytes and other Indians didn't always go along meekly with the desires of the Spanish missionaries. During the mission period, nearly every mission suffered an Indian uprising.

In the fall of 1775, a serious revolt took place in San Diego. People of the Kumeyaay tribe were very reluctant to give up their old way of life. Just after midnight on November 5, about 800 Kumeyaay from at least 15 villages banded together and attacked. They looted storerooms and burned the wooden mission buildings. They didn't attack the presidio, but the soldiers there slept through the revolt and didn't help the missionaries. During the attack, three Spaniards were killed, including a 35-year-old missionary. A new mission would not be built at the site until 1777.

In 1781, Yuma tribes rose up, killing 34 Spaniards and destroying two missions on the Colorado River. This revolt against Spanish missionaries and settlers resulted in the closing of the Anza Trail (part of El Camino Real) for 40 years, cutting off communication between Mexico and California.

The most serious Indian revolt in California's mission history took place in 1824. Hundreds of neophytes, angry with poor treatment and hard labor, rose up at Mission La Purísima, at present-day Lompoc, and at Mission Santa Barbara. At La Purísima, the neophytes burned buildings to the ground. In Santa Barbara, 2,000 Indians temporarily took control of the mission.

Other neophytes tried to escape their captivity. In 1795, for example, more than 200 Indians escaped from the missions. According to some estimates, as many as 15 percent of all neophytes attempted to run away.

The missionaries were hard on those who attempted to escape. Runaways were hunted down and punished by being whipped or locked up. Those neophytes who became violent were forced to do hard labor or executed. In 1806, German visitor Georg von Langsdorff described the usual outcome of such escape attempts: "*[The runaway] is almost always brought back to the misión, where . . . an iron rod a foot-and-a-half long and an inch in diameter is fastened to one of his feet. This . . . prevents the Indian from making another attempt to escape, and has the effect of terrifying the others.*"

Soldiers carrying whips manage groups of Indians getting ready to work at the San Francisco presidio in northern California. Parts of the presidio, built in 1776, still stand today.

Over the years, the missions would prove an economic success. For the Native Americans, however, the missions were a social tragedy. ❋

CHAPTER FOUR

Presidios and Pueblos

SPANISH SOLDIERS AND SETTLERS *forge a new life on the frontier of Spain's newest colony.*

While the goal of the missionary was to convert California's Indians to Christianity, the goal of the presidio soldier was to protect the mission and to strengthen Spain's claim to California. During the Spanish colonial period, four strategically located presidios were built to protect Spanish missions and the settlers who lived there. These presidios were San Diego (1769), Monterey (1770), San Francisco (1776), and Santa Barbara (1786). Until 1848, these four forts offered the only protection for the Spanish in California.

OPPOSITE: This print, based on an 1816 watercolor, shows Native American men at a mission engaged in a game of chance. Although gambling was popular among the Indians, it was prohibited by the friars. Neophytes who were caught gambling were often punished.

A pueblo near the Mission of Saint Joseph was a simple place settled by the wives of soldiers stationed at the nearby presidio and other families who had traveled from Mexico. They hoped to make new lives for themselves with the offer of free land and supplies.

New Spain was interested in maintaining only a military presence, not a strong military power, in California. The Spanish colony already had to station soldiers in other parts of New Spain, including Mexico and parts of the present-day Southwest region of the United States. As far as Spanish officials were concerned, California was a very low priority. As a result, there were never many troops in the colony at one time. The presidios themselves were often poorly constructed, damp, and uncomfortable. In 1792, English explorer and California visitor George Vancouver described the commander's home:

The floor was of native soil raised about three feet from its original level, without being boarded, paved, or even reduced to an even surface. The roof was covered in with flags [the leaves

> *of a plant] and rushes; the walls on the inside had once been whitewashed; the furniture consisted of a very sparing assortment of the most indispensable articles, of the rudest fashion and of the meanest kind; and ill-accorded with the ideas we had conceived of the sumptuous manner in which the Spaniards live on this side of the globe.*

He continued, "*There is not an object to indicate the most remote connection with any European or other civilized nation.*"

To make matters worse, the poorly trained soldiers often lacked important supplies—such as gunpowder—needed to defend the colony. Their pay was low and often slow in coming. Despite these shortcomings, the presidios did serve to intimidate the Indians of the region. And for many years, the Spanish military presence was enough of a deterrent to keep away foreign invaders.

An Uneasy Relationship

Conflict between missionaries and soldiers was common. While the missionaries were in charge of the religious life in the colony, the presidio commanders were in charge of the military and political processes. The missionaries had no direct authority over the soldiers, and the presidio commander had no authority over the missions.

Friar Luis Jayme, head of the San Diego mission, wrote: "*Little progress will be made under present conditions . . . very many of them [the soldiers] deserve to be hanged on account of the continuous outrages which they are committing in seizing and raping the [Indian] women.*" The missionaries also complained that the soldiers encouraged the neophytes to gamble and drink alcohol, and antagonized, assaulted, and even murdered local unconverted Indians.

Adding to problems between the missionaries and the soldiers was the presidio's growing dependence upon mission goods. In the early days of settlement, both missions and presidios had relied on the supply ships from Mexico for food and other goods. But the supply ships were unreliable, and as the missions flourished, the presidios came to depend upon them. The missions sold soap, clothing, shoes, blankets, candles, and wine to the residents of the presidio. The mission ranches supplied the soldiers with food.

The relationship wasn't totally one-sided. The missionaries counted on the presidio soldiers to round up escaped neophytes. And the credits that they got from the soldiers for food and other goods could be exchanged for luxuries such as spices, chocolate, fine wine, and prayer books. Instead of receiving cash for pay, presidio soldiers were often given credit to purchase goods from the presidio storehouse. The missionaries, in turn, used the credits when sending letters to Mexico City requesting these luxury items, which were then sent on the supply ships to the missions.

One of the most bitter disputes between a missionary and a soldier was the feud between Father Junípero Serra and California's military governor, Pedro Fages. Fages, a tough military leader known to beat men who didn't work hard enough, insisted that he was in charge of California and that everyone else—even missionaries—should follow his orders. He angered Serra by refusing to create more missions until New Spain sent enough soldiers to protect the new settlements adequately. The two Spaniards also feuded over food and other supplies, land, and control of the neophytes.

By 1773, Serra had had enough. He traveled to Mexico City and submitted a 32-point written complaint to New Spain's new viceroy. His visit was effective: The viceroy demoted Fages, and he was removed from office in 1774. The viceroy also promised to send doctors, carpenters, and supplies to the missions.

The First Pueblos

In 1773, four years after the founding of San Diego's mission and presidio, the total Spanish population in Alta California was 72. Officials in New Spain knew that more colonists were needed to make California a successful colony. The answer, they believed, was to found pueblos, or villages, near existing Spanish missions and presidios. These pueblos could also serve as a new source of food and goods for the presidios, allowing the soldiers to

pueblo—a village, not associated with a mission, founded in California

lessen their reliance on the missions. To populate the pueblos, soldiers would be encouraged to bring their wives. Officials hoped that this would reduce the number of assaults against Native American women.

The first independent pueblo was El Pueblo de San José de Guadalupe, or San José, founded in 1777 by Felipe de Neve, California's first civil (nonmilitary) governor. The new town was located between the presidios of San Francisco and Monterey. The first settlers were fourteen volunteers who had been living temporarily at the two presidios, along with their families. Within the first few years of settlement, San José was doing well, growing enough wheat to supply the two nearby presidios. By 1848, the town had a population of 700.

One of de Neve's last acts as governor was to found El Pueblo de Nuestra Señora la Reina de Los Angeles in 1781. The town, located near Mission San Gabriel Arcángel, was initially called El Pueblo, but later became known as Los Angeles. The first colonists were 44 poor, mainly illiterate people, most of African or Native American ancestry, from northern Mexico. They had been enticed to the new settlement with the offer of free land and supplies. Although the new Los Angeles residents were considered lazy drunkards by missionaries at San Gabriel, in reality they worked hard. Within ten years of the pueblo's founding, Los Angeles produced more grain than any other settlement in California.

The founding in 1781 of Los Angeles, one of California's first pueblos, is dramatized in this engraving by friars, neophytes, soldiers, and Mexican settlers joining in prayer and musical celebration.

The last of California's three independent pueblos was the Villa de Branciforte, founded in 1797. Located near present-day Santa Cruz, this pueblo was the least successful. It was supposed to be a home for retired soldiers and their families, but none would come to California to live.

Instead, the pueblo housed criminals who had been banished to New Spain's northern colony. The Villa de Branciforte did not thrive, and five years after its founding, the government stopped funding it.

PROFILE

Eulalia Callis de Fages

In 1781, Pedro Fages replaced Felipe de Neve as California's civil governor. His wife, Eulalia Callis de Fages, arrived in California two years later. She was the first First Lady to take up residence in the Spanish colony. Callis quickly became known for her generous nature and kindness to the Indians. She gave away her own and her husband's clothing and tended people who were ill. However, Callis hated the rough, rugged colonial lifestyle. Before long, she told her husband that she wanted to take her children and return to Mexico. When he refused, she banned him from their home for three months.

When Callis publicly demanded a divorce, the governor had the missionaries take her to Mission San Carlos, where she was locked up for several months. The priests promised to handcuff, beat, and excommunicate her if she didn't change her ways. Eventually, the couple reconciled. They remained together in California until 1790, when they returned to Mexico. Pedro Fages died in 1794.

alcalde—Spanish colonial official in charge of a pueblo, similar to a town's mayor

ayuntamiento—a pueblo's governing council

regidore—member of a pueblo's governing council

Each pueblo was headed by an *alcalde.* Although the citizens of each pueblo elected the alcalde, the governor of California had to approve their choice. The alcalde relied on the *ayuntamiento* to assist him in governing the pueblo and the surrounding area. The *regidores* created laws to manage the pueblo.

By the early 1790s, the Spanish-speaking population in California had increased to about 970 people, a large increase over the past 20 years. The growing colony would soon attract the attention of foreign powers. One nation that would take an interest in California was the United States of America. In 1790, Rhode Island became the last of the 13 original British colonies on the East Coast to ratify the Constitution. In the coming decades, the new nation would grow and prosper, and American citizens would begin pushing westward in search of land and new opportunities. U.S. officials would also look for ways to expand American territory farther and farther west. ✻

CHAPTER FIVE

A Remote Colony

As officials in New Spain try to quell a rebellion in Mexico, settlers in California welcome foreign traders.

In the early days of Spanish settlement in California, few foreigners visited the colony. Then, in 1792, English explorer George Vancouver, in his ship *Discovery*, became the first non-Spanish person to visit San Francisco Bay. Vancouver was putting his crew and himself in danger: By Spanish decree, trade with foreigners was forbidden in California, and the captain risked having his ship impounded and his crew jailed. However, Spanish authorities were far away in Mexico,

OPPOSITE: George Vancouver's *Voyage of Discovery*, a book describing his exploration of San Francisco, includes this engraving of the Mission San Carlos Borromeo near Monterey. Domed huts in the background sheltered the neophytes, while the simple church and storehouse were built around crops tended by the Native Americans and friars of the mission.

and the Englishman was welcomed with open arms by officials and soldiers who remained in San Francisco.

He and his men stayed in the region for two months, becoming familiar with the presidio, nearby missions, and the surrounding countryside. Vancouver found it hard to believe the state of the Indians. He wrote, *"I was astonished to observe how few advantages had attended their conversion."* He continued, *"All the operations and functions, both body and mind, appeared to be carried on with a mechanical, lifeless, careless indifference."* The Spanish told him that the Indians had always acted that way.

George Vancouver's *Discovery* and Spanish sailing ships anchored off what is now called Vancouver Island in British Columbia, Canada

Vancouver reported to British naval officials that the colony, with its poor defenses and sparse development, would be easy for Britain to conquer. He criticized the Spanish for failing to take advantage of a land that had so many natural advantages—excellent harbors, fertile soil, and a warm climate. Vancouver visited San Francisco three times between 1792 and 1794. His book, *A Voyage of Discovery,* enticed foreign ships to visit California and people to settle there. It also provided a look at life in the early California missions.

THE RUSSIANS ARRIVE

In 1765, rumors of Russian hunters off the coast of San Francisco had prompted the Spanish to settle California. In the early 1800s, northern trading posts in Alaska were operated by the Russian-American Company, a hunting and trading business. Although the waters off the coast of Alaska were rich in fur-bearing mammals, the climate and soil of the region were not good for growing food crops.

At first, the Russian traders and trappers relied on supply ships. But in 1805, when no supply ship from Russia arrived at the trading post in Sitka, Alaska, the residents were forced to eat eagles, crows, and anything they could pull out of the sea. The Russians soon became sick with scurvy. Officials of the company realized that they needed to take action to save their money-making outposts.

In 1806, merchant-explorer and Russian-American Company official Nikolai Petrovich Rezanov arrived in San Francisco. Rezanov was desperate to establish a trading relationship with the Spanish. Without such a relationship, the survival of his company's trading post in Sitka was in jeopardy.

At first, Spanish colonists refused to trade with Rezanov and his men. The Spanish also refused to allow Rezanov to travel to Monterey to visit California's governor, José de Arrillaga. Later, the Russian would write, *"Thereupon I recognized the suspicious nature of the Spanish government, which at every point prevents foreign visitors from gaining knowledge of the interior of the country and from observing the weakness of their military defenses."*

Preventing Desertion

Rezanov was convinced that some of his men, weary of the harsh conditions in Alaska, would prefer to stay in the mild climate of California. So he took special precautions. His shipmate, German scientist Georg von Langsdorff, recorded that Rezanov first ordered that three men who had requested to remain behind were sent to a

> *barren island, where they were held until the day of our departure. [Next,] we placed pickets on shore and established rounds [a schedule], and a mounted patrol [soldiers on horseback] was given us by the Spaniards; but, in spite of every precaution, two of our most esteemed men, Mikhail Kalianin and Peter Polkanov, seized the opportunity to escape when at the creek washing their clothes, vanishing without a trace.*

During his stay in San Francisco, Rezanov became enchanted by the 15-year-old daughter of the presidio's commander. His shipmate, Georg von Langsdorff, recalled, "*The bright, sparkling eyes of Doña Concepción had made a deep impression and pierced his inmost soul. He conceived the idea that through a marriage with the daughter of the commandante of the Presidio de San Francisco a close bond would be formed for future business intercourse between the Russian-American Company and the provincia of Nueva California.*" Langsdorff wrote that Rezanov decided to "sacrifice himself" for the good of his country by proposing to the teenager.

Nikolai Rezanov

Although her parents did not approve, Concepción Argüello accepted the Russian's proposal of marriage. Perhaps she wanted a life outside of California. According to Rezanov, she referred to her home as "*a beautiful country, a warm climate, an abundance of grain and cattle—and nothing else.*" Or perhaps she was charmed by the older, dashing, and world-wise Russian. After the engagement, the Spanish were indeed more helpful. They offered the Russians loads of bread, dried meat, and other supplies to take back to Sitka.

The meeting and engagement was the beginning of trade between the two nations. In the coming years, ships from both nations would travel to each other's ports in the New World.

An Ill-Fated ROMANCE

IN MAY 1806, REZANOV LEFT CALIFORNIA, PROMISING TO secure permission from his church to marry his Spanish fiancée. He stopped at Sitka, where he dropped off food and supplies. Then he set sail for Siberia in northeastern Russia. As he was crossing Siberia, Rezanov caught pneumonia. He died on March 1, 1807.

Concepción Argüello did not immediately hear of her fiancé's death. For several years, she awaited news of him. Finally, an officer who had accompanied Rezanov through Siberia visited California and gave her the bad news. Although her parents encouraged her to marry, Concepción chose instead to become a nun. She spent the rest of her life doing good deeds. She is buried in Benicia, California.

BELOW: Before becoming a nun, Concepción Argüello wore this mantilla, or short lace scarf, and comb as a headdress, typical of Spanish women at that time.

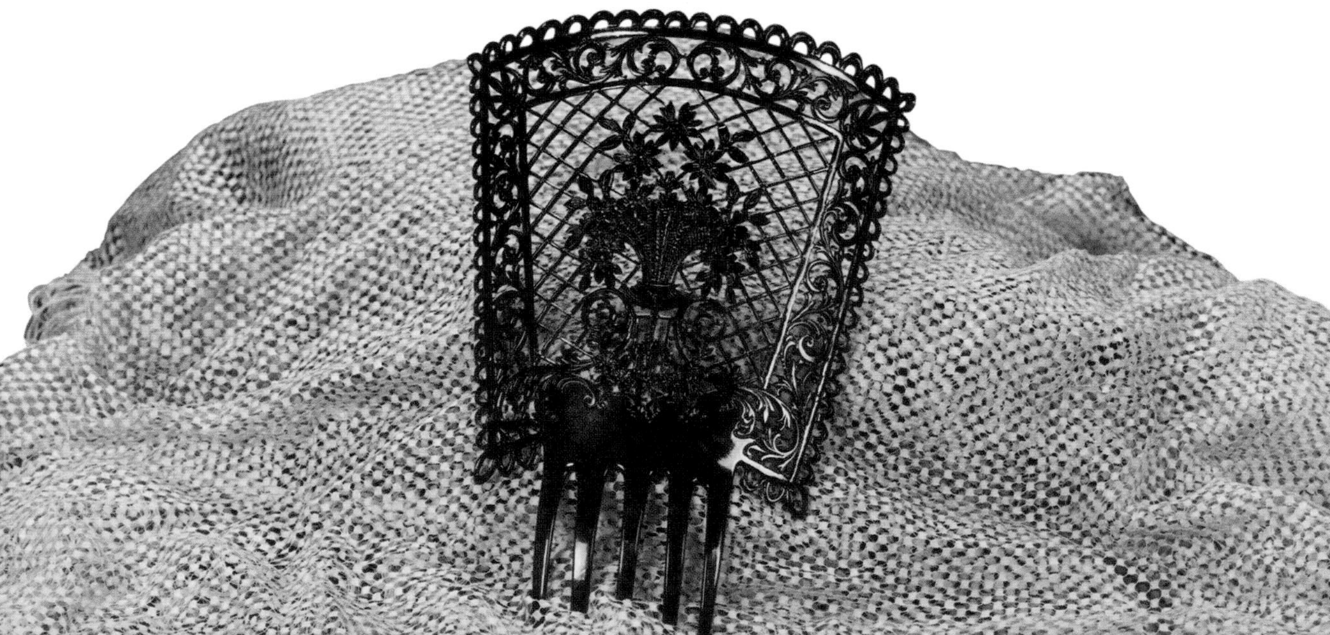

Unrest in New Spain

In 1810, Mexico began its struggle for independence from Spain. Mexico was following in the footsteps of other Spanish colonies in the New World that had begun fighting for their freedom. Over the next 11 years, the people of Mexico battled violently to be free from Spain.

The rebellion in Mexico had some immediate effects upon California. As Spanish officials in New Spain focused on winning the war, financial and other support for California came to a halt. Supply ships stopped arriving, and missionaries and soldiers were not paid.

The missions, now self-sustaining, were able to weather the tough times. They were able to support the four presidios and three pueblos as well. During these times of need, however, some of the missionaries were stingy, offering only the most basic supplies to the presidio soldiers. A French scientist taking part in a Russian expedition to California in 1816 wrote about the effects on those living at the presidio in San Francisco:

> *The misery in which they had been wallowing for six to seven years, forgotten and forsaken by Mexico, the motherland, did not permit them to be hosts. . . . They spoke only with bitterness of the missionaries, who in the face of a deficiency in imported goods nonetheless enjoyed a superfluity of the products of the earth and would let them have nothing now that their money had run out, except in return for a promissory note—and, even*

> *so, only what is absolutely necessary to maintain life, among which things bread and flour are not included. For years they had lived on maize, without seeing bread."*

With Spanish officials focusing on problems in New Spain, they had less time to enforce trade restrictions within California. This opened the door to increased foreign trade there. The Russians weren't the only outsiders to enter California in the early 1800s. American and British trading ships began arriving more regularly, and California's officials turned a blind eye to the illegal trading. As Governor and Presidio Commander José Dario Argüello said, "*Necessity makes licit [legal] what is not licit by law.*"

Fort Ross

In 1812, the Russians, taking advantage of the chaos in New Spain, founded their own outpost in California. In March, the Russian-American Company, under license from the Russian tsar, built two colonies. The first was located at Bodega Bay, north of San Francisco, for hunting purposes. The second, Fort Ross, was sited 18 miles (29 km) north. Fort Ross, it was hoped, would serve as both a trading post and a place to grow food supplies.

The first settlers at Fort Ross included about 95 Russians and 80 Aleutians—immediately making the new settlement larger than any existing presidio. The settlers constructed their fortress on the site of an old Indian village, at the mouth of the present-day Russian River in Sonoma County. The new outpost included two blockhouses that could house 40 cannon for the fort's defense. The colonists also built storehouses, barracks, a windmill, a bakery, and bathhouses. Nearby, they built a shipyard, tannery, forge, and boathouse.

Fort Ross, home to Russian and Aleutian trappers and traders, was a large, thriving trading post and Russia's southernmost settlement in North America. It was the site of California's first windmills and shipbuilding yards and included a chapel, a stockade, barracks, and blockhouses. The settlement lasted almost 30 years.

Soon after the fort was founded, Spanish troops arrived and asked the Russians to leave. The Russians politely refused, but offered to begin trading with the

Spanish. When Governor Argüello realized that the Russians would be difficult to dislodge, he decided that a trading relationship might be beneficial, especially now that supplies from New Spain were running low.

Other Visitors

The first Americans to see Spanish California were sailors on board merchant vessels from the East. In 1816, a crew member of the trading ship *Albatross* became California's first American settler. Thomas W. Doak decided to stay behind when his ship left Monterey, where he put his carpentry skills to good use. Doak converted to Catholicism and married a local woman. He was even hired to paint the altar of Mission San Juan Bautista. As more American boats pulled into California ports, other sailors followed Doak's example.

Not all foreign visits to California were harmless. In November 1818, a French privateer named Hippolyte Bouchard invaded Monterey. Bouchard, who said he was there to advance the freedom of Mexico, set fire to the settlement. The following month, the pirates moved on to Mission San Juan Capistrano, which they also partially destroyed. Then Bouchard and his crew abruptly sailed away, never to return.

privateer—a pirate who is licensed or sanctioned by a government to attack enemy ships for money and goods

PROFILE

Joseph Chapman

Born in Maine, Joseph Chapman was in the Sandwich Islands (present-day Hawaii) when the pirate Hippolyte Bouchard forced him into service. During the pirates' raid on Monterey, Chapman was captured and imprisoned by the Spanish. After he was released from jail, he remained in Monterey and helped build mills and mission buildings there. In 1822, Chapman converted to Catholicism, married a Spanish woman, and started a family. Two years later, he gave up his American citizenship to become a naturalized citizen of Mexico. Chapman died in 1848, on the eve of great changes in his adopted country.

By 1820, the sight of foreign traders in California ports, although still officially illegal, was no longer a novelty. Despite the struggles in New Spain, California was managing to survive. In all, more than 24,000 people lived in the Spanish missions, presidios, and pueblos. Spanish California had weathered some changes over the past few years, but even greater challenges lay ahead. ❋

Changing Hands

UNDER MEXICAN RULE, *California's missions are closed, and American settlers are welcomed.*

In September 1821, Mexico won its independence from Spain. California, now part of the new Republic of Mexico, didn't get the news for seven months. For most Californios, the news made little immediate difference. People in the northern colony—Alta California—had not taken part in the struggle for freedom, and most had remained loyal to Spain. They did, however, expect from Mexico the financial support and supplies that they had received in the past from New Spain.

OPPOSITE: This painting by famed American artist Frederic Remington shows Jedediah Strong Smith and his men crossing the desert. He was the first American to reach Mexican territory by land from the east.

In 1824, Mexico's first constitution went into effect. Under the new government structure, people in California were allowed an advisory legislature made up of Californios. They were also given a governor appointed in Mexico City. The advisory legislature could suggest rules, which were then sent to Mexico for approval. The territory was officially controlled, however, by Mexico's new Congress.

Californios—Mexican settlers in California

The first Mexican governor in California was José María Echeandía. Echeandía, who arrived in 1825, chose to make San Diego his home and, by default, California's capital.

Giving Out Land

The new government in Mexico was ready to give out land throughout California. Mexican officials believed that the old Spanish policy of granting land only to missions was unfair. Ranchers who agreed to settle on the land were awarded huge stretches of territory. The first such grant was given in 1823 to Captain Francisco María Ruíz. Ruíz called his 8,486-acre (3,437-ha) ranch Los Peñasquitos ("Little Hills"). In the coming years, the Mexican government would make 33 land grants, covering 948 square miles (2,455 sq km). Even Americans and other foreign nationals, once they converted to Catholicism and became Mexican citizens, were awarded pieces of California.

An important part of Mexico's land grant plan was the decision to secularize the Franciscan missions. This meant that the government planned to take control of the missions away from the Catholic Church and give the land and livestock to California residents and converted natives. The process of turning California's 21 missions into *ranchos* began in 1833 under California's new governor, José Luís Figueroa. In August, Figueroa announced that the 18,000 neophytes were no longer bound to the missions. He also began dividing up the millions of acres of mission land.

secularize—to transfer from religious to civil control

rancho—a ranch

According to the new law, each neophyte was supposed to receive a small parcel of land that had once been mission land. However, most of the neophytes were never given this information, and the best mission lands were given to Californios or to people of Spanish descent who had just arrived from Mexico. In all, 700 private land grants were eventually made of former mission land, usually around 15,000 acres (6,075 ha) each.

The situation of the former neophytes went from bad to worse. Most ended up working for the *rancheros,* the powerful new class of white landowners. Lansford W. Hastings, who wrote *The Emigrants' Guide to Oregon and California* in 1845, described the condition of the Native Americans: "*The natives . . . in California . . . are in a state of*

ranchero—under Mexican rule, a rancher who controlled large stretches of land in California

absolute vassalage [slavery], even more degrading, and more oppressive than that of our slaves in the south. . . .It is quite certain, that the labors of Indians will, for many years, be as little expensive to the farmers of that country, as slave labor."

After a day of herding cattle, vaqueros gather at the entrance of a thatched hut, their home on the ranch of their employers. The cowboys wore full capes and hats typical of Spanish dress at the time.

Indians who did manage to get hold of a piece of land were often murdered or driven away by groups of Californios. In 1837, José María Amador described one such posse:

> *The troops, the civilians, and the auxiliaries surrounded [the Native Americans] and tied them up . . . we separated 100 Christians. At every half mile or mile we put six of them on their knees to say their prayers, making them understand that they were about to die. Each one was shot with four arrows. . . . Those who refused to die immediately were killed with*

spears. . . .We baptized all the Indians (non-Christians) and afterward they were shot in the back.

The missions, soon deserted, came to reflect the tragic life of the Indians. Edwin Bryant, who spent the night at Mission San José in 1846, wrote,

I passed through extensive warehouses and immense rooms, once occupied for the manufacture of woollen blankets and other articles, with the rude machinery still standing in them, but unemployed. Filth and desolation have taken the place of cleanliness and busy life. . . .These ruinous missions are prolific generators, and the nurseries of vermin of all kinds, as the hapless traveller who tarries in them a few hours will learn to his sorrow.

American Seamen and Merchants

Another important change in California was a new, relaxed trade policy. Americans and other foreign visitors were now welcomed in California ports. The year after Mexican independence, the number of ships visiting California more than doubled from 9 to 20. By 1826, that number had risen to 44.

One of the first Americans to take advantage of this new, merchant-friendly atmosphere was William Alden Gale from Boston, who worked for a trading firm called Bryant & Sturgis. In 1822, Gale secured a monopoly on the hide and tallow business in California by paying two dollars each for

"Yankee dollars," cured cow hides that were sent back East and made into shoes. Gale also opened a general store, selling tools, furniture, and toys as well as such exotic goods such as fireworks, music boxes, and satin cloth.

Another early arrival was hide and tallow merchant Alfred Robinson. A young man from Boston who arrived in California in 1829, Robinson married a Spanish woman and stayed in his adopted home for the rest of his life. In 1846, he published *Life in California,* a book that encouraged Americans to head West. The book described life at the missions and ranchos, the weak Mexican government in the colony, the Californios, and the ever-growing number of Americans. However, it also strengthened ethnic stereotypes against the Spanish. Robinson often referred to Californios as "indolent," or lazy. Like other Americans, Robinson believed that California would thrive under some other government: *"A country like California requires robust and enterprising men—accustomed to labor in the field, and to a life of simplicity and economy."*

tallow—a liquid made from cow fat that was used in soaps and candles and as a lubricant for wagon wheels

The Mountain Men

Another group of Americans who began arriving in the late 1820s was the mountain men. These fur trappers lived in the Rocky Mountains year-round, earning a living by trapping beavers in the rivers and lakes.

The first of these independent trappers to visit California was Jedediah Strong Smith. In 1826, he became the first American to reach the Mexican territory from the east by land instead of by ship. Smith forged a trail from the Salt Lake Valley in present-day Utah through the Mojave Desert to Mission San Gabriel, near San Diego. He later submitted a report about the geography of California to the U.S. Secretary of War.

In the coming years, many more Yankee fur trappers and traders visited California. By scouting overland passages to California from the east, the mountain men played an invaluable role in American settlement of the western coast.

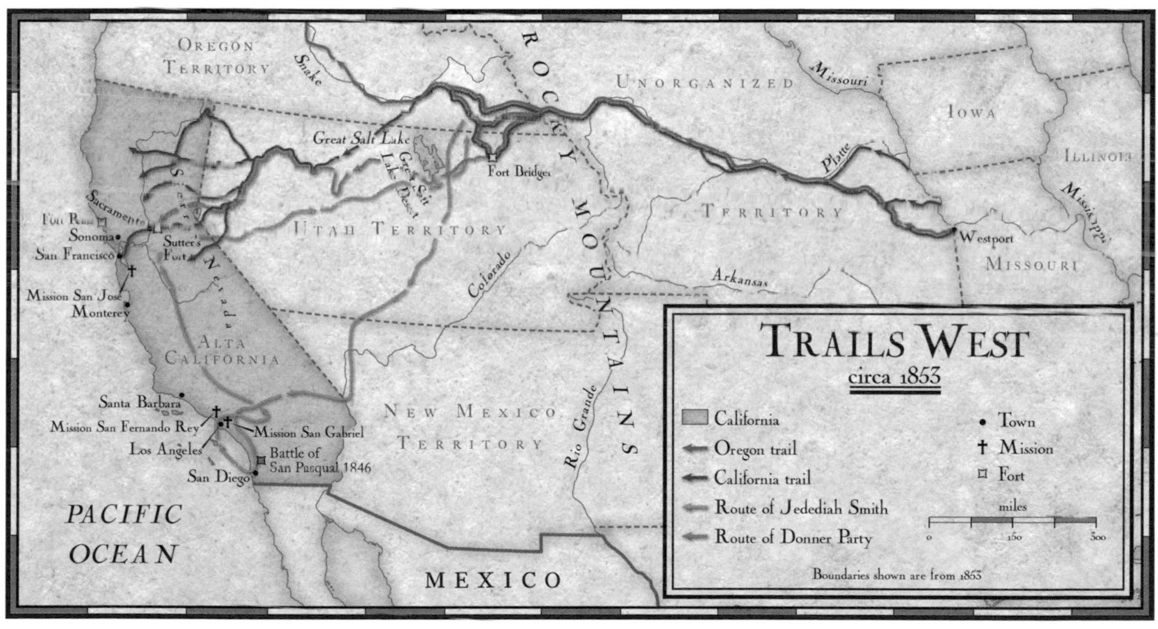

More than 20 years after mountain man Jedediah Smith (yellow route) arrived, California was invaded by thousands seeking to make their fortunes in the goldfields. Most traveling overland headed west along the Oregon Trail before turning south and west, following what became known as the California Trail (red route). As the Donner Party (green route) discovered, it was a dangerous journey.

The American Migration Begins

In the mid- and late 1830s, more and more Americans went to California. Some, like Richard Henry Dana of Boston, just visited. Dana, a Harvard student, left school and signed on with the trading ship *Pilgrim* for a two-year trip around Cape Horn to California. During the 1834–1836 trip, the ship docked at a number of ports in California, and Dana worked hauling "Yankee dollars" from shore to ship. He also spent four months in San Diego, writing that the region was *"blessed with a climate than which there can be no better in the world."*

In 1840, after returning to Boston, Dana published an account of his trip in a book called *Two Years Before the Mast: A Personal Narrative of Life at Sea*. Dana thought California was a beautiful, fertile place, and the Californios were not making the most of it. He wrote, *"In the hands of an enterprising people, what a country this might be!"* Dana's book encouraged Americans to migrate to California.

In 1841, the first organized wagon train of American settlers arrived in Mexican California. Called the Bidwell-Bartelson party, the group was sponsored by the Western Emigration Society, founded by mountain man Antoine Robidoux. The group of 69 men, women, and children had left Westport, Missouri, on May 18. The party was led along the Oregon Trail by a mountain man named Thomas "Old Broken Hand" Fitzpatrick.

mountain man—a fur trapper who lived and hunted in the mountains of the West

New Helvetia

By 1840, the Russians had abandoned Fort Ross. Sea otters and seals in the region were nearly hunted out, and the fort was not the food source for Alaska that Russia had hoped. The following year, the Russians sold the outpost to John Sutter, a Swiss immigrant who traveled the West as a fur trader. The Russians also sold Sutter 48,000 acres (19,440 ha) in the Sacramento Valley. Here, Sutter founded New Helvetia (New Switzerland), a settlement with a fort, cattle ranch, crops, orchards, and vineyards. He also hired American immigrants and provided aid to travelers trying to cross the Sierras. In 1848, Sutter hired James Marshall to build a sawmill about 40 miles (64 km) upriver from Sutter's Fort. Sutter's Mill, as the sawmill would be known, was located on the south fork of the American River. When completed, it would provide the lumber needed to build a flour mill and other important buildings in New Helvetia. It would also be the site of an event that would rewrite California history.

PROFILE

The Donner Party

Migrating to California could be very dangerous. Some groups of migrants seemed plagued with bad luck from the start. One such group was the Donner Party.

Made up of 81 men, women, and children—including George and Jacob Donner and their families—the group began their trip to California in April 1846. In June, their guide quit. In August, the party ran low on food while crossing the Great Salt Lake Desert. In October, they got lost in the Sierra Nevada, and then were stranded in the snowy mountains when the weather worsened. Over time, 41 people died from starvation, cold, and other dangers. By the end of December, the desperate survivors had resorted to eating the bodies of their dead traveling companions.

The 48 survivors of the Donner Party were finally rescued in January by a group out of Sutter's Fort. Thirteen-year-old survivor Virginia Reed offered the following advice to her cousin back East,

O Mary I have not wrote you half of the truble we have had but I hav Wrote you anuf to let you now that you dont now what truble is . . . but Dont let this letter dishaten anybody and never take no cutofs and hury along as fast as you can.

In Idaho, the Bidwell-Bartelson party split up. Half continued on to Oregon, while the other half—32 men, one woman, and a baby—followed the Humboldt River toward California along a pathway that would become known as the California Trail. They arrived in the Sacramento Valley on November 4. The only woman in this group was an 18-year-old pregnant mother, Nancy Kelsey. The first American woman in California, she had refused to allow her husband, Ben, to leave her and their baby daughter Ann behind. *"Where my husband goes, I go," she said. "I can better stand the hardships of the journey than the anxieties for an absent husband."*

The overland route from Missouri to California was not easy. The route measured about 2,000 miles (3,218 km) and could take up to five months, depending upon the weather, Indian attacks, and other factors. Many of those who set out to make a new life for themselves in California never arrived. According to some estimates, as many as 20,000 people died along the way.

These new American migrants were very different from the Americans who had come before. These new arrivals brought their families, refused to learn Spanish, and remained Protestant citizens of the United States. In the coming years, the population of English-speaking settlers, who considered themselves "American" not Californian, would continue to grow. And they would become more and more dissatisfied living under Mexican rule. ※

CHAPTER SEVEN

Life in Mexican California

THE RANCHEROS GAIN LAND—*and power—in Mexican California.*

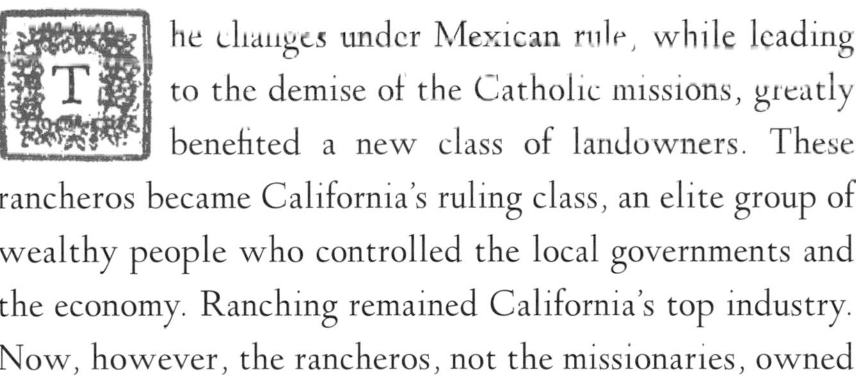

The changes under Mexican rule, while leading to the demise of the Catholic missions, greatly benefited a new class of landowners. These rancheros became California's ruling class, an elite group of wealthy people who controlled the local governments and the economy. Ranching remained California's top industry. Now, however, the rancheros, not the missionaries, owned

OPPOSITE: Rancheros lasso a steer on one of the large ranches where huge herds of cattle roamed freely. By the late 1700s, ranching had become the leading industry of California.

the land and huge herds of cattle. Now permitted to trade freely with foreign merchants, the rancheros grew rich in the hide and tallow business.

As in mission days, the cattle and sheep were allowed to roam freely over the land. Once a year, vaqueros, usually former neophytes, would round up the livestock to be branded or slaughtered. The *matanza* was often held in the fall, and as many as a hundred cows were slaughtered at once.

matanza—the yearly slaughtering of cattle on the ranchos

The ranchos were kept running by Native American labor. In 1835, Richard Henry Dana wrote, "*The Indians . . . do all the hard work, two or three being attached to the better house [wealthier rancheros]; and the poorest persons are able to keep one [Indian], at least, for they have only to feed them, and give them a small piece of coarse cloth and a belt, for the men, and a coarse gown, without shoes or stockings, for the women.*" Indian workers were treated better by some rancheros than others. Unscrupulous Californios sometimes tricked the Indians into working for nearly nothing. Others raided Indian villages and enslaved the natives.

One Mexican woman washes clothes while another carries a water jug on her head at a watering hole on a rancho in Southern California. The man watching is likely overseeing the domestic workers doing chores for the ranchero.

GETTING AROUND

IN A REGION WHERE ROADS WERE ROUGH AND MOST RANCHOS were located miles from the nearest pueblo, horses were an important part of life. In California, horses were the chief way that men, women, and children got from one place to another. Even business was conducted from the back of a horse. It's not surprising that one visitor to California remarked that the Californios were probably the best riders in the world.

In 1846, Edwin Bryant described how people in California managed to get around so quickly:

A gentleman who starts upon a journey of 100 miles [161 km] and wishes to perform the trip in a day will take with him ten fresh horses and a vaquero. The eight loose horses are placed under the charge of the vaquero, and are driven in front, at the rate of ten or twelve miles [16 or 19 km] an hour. . . . At the end of twenty miles [32 km], the horses that have been rode are discharged, and turned into the caballada [herd], and horses that have not been rode, but driven along without weight, are saddled and mounted and rode at the same speed, and so on to the end of the journey. If a horse gives out from inability to proceed at this gait, he is left on the road. The owner's brand is on him, and if of any value, he can be recovered without difficulty.

Under the rancheros, grain growing and wine making also flourished. However, the rancheros and their families came to rely on foreign merchants—especially American ones—for most material goods. (At this time, the United States was still a foreign nation to people in Mexican California.) Taking advantage of the rancheros' desire for foreign furniture and clothing and the fact that they had little competition, American traders charged three times what someone in Boston would have paid for the same item.

The wife of a wealthy ranchero would dress in expensive clothes imported from Spain and other areas of Europe. This woman wears a hand-carved comb in her hair and a shawl of fine cloth draped over her shoulders.

The wives of the rancheros were especially fond of the clothing brought to them from foreign ports. Dana reported,

> *The fondness for dress among the women is excessive, and is sometimes their ruin. A present of a fine mantle, or of a necklace or pair of ear-rings, gains the favor of the greater part. Nothing is more common than to see a woman living in a house of only two rooms, with the ground for a floor, dressed in spangled satin shoes, silk gown, high comb, and gilt, if not gold, ear-rings and necklace.*

The trading ships that traveled from one California port to another also delivered mail and carried visitors and other travelers. As a result, stops by the ships were something to look forward to, and the ship's officers were welcomed and often grandly entertained.

The Founding of *San Francisco*

In 1835, a tiny trading post was founded east of the presidio at San Francisco. The town, called Yerba Buena, began with just a single tent. As the home of the growing tallow trade and with its prime location at San Francisco's port, Yerba Buena grew quickly. Before long, houses, shops, and saloons were popping up everywhere. In February 1847, Edwin Bryant wrote, "*The little village . . . is fast becoming a town of importance.*" In 1847, after the Americans took control of the town, Yerba Buena was renamed San Francisco.

The Rancheros

Among the ranching families, the father was the head of the household. The children were expected to behave and to be obedient to both their parents. Wives were also expected to honor and obey their husbands. Men, in turn, were expected to treat their wives with respect. In Mexican California, women were given some protection from abusive husbands. One man named Higuera was punished for cutting his wife's hair off in a jealous rage.

Men were in charge of the management of the rancho, while women were expected to care for the home. Some women, however, managed their own ranchos. Under the Mexican government, at least 66 land grants went to women in California, most of whom were single or widowed. One such grant went to Maria Lopez-Carillo, born in California in 1792. After the death of her husband, Lopez-Carillo moved to Sonoma Valley and learned how to farm. She also learned how to speak the language of the region's Indians so she could talk to her vaqueros. In 1841, the governor gave her nearly 9,000 acres (3,654 ha) in her own name. On her rancho, Cabeza de Santa Rosa, Lopez-Carillo had about 3,000 cattle. She also grew grain, vegetables, and fruit.

Most of the rancheros lived in modest houses, usually made of adobe. Richard Henry Dana wrote,

> *The houses here [in Monterey], as everywhere else in California, are of one story, built of adobes, that is clay made into large bricks, about a foot and a half square, and three or four inches thick, and hardened in the sun. These are joined together by a cement of the same material, and the whole are of a common dirt-color. The floors are generally of earth, the windows grated [barred] and without glass; and the doors, which are seldom shut, open directly into the common room, there being no entries [entry foyers]. Some of the more wealthy inhabitants have glass to their windows and board floors; and in Monterey nearly all the houses are plastered on the outside.*

Ranching families looked forward to such social events as weddings and holiday celebrations. Because the distance between ranchos was often great, the festivities stretched out for days at a time. A typical celebration included lots of food, drinking, and dancing.

Dana described attending a wedding dance he attended in Santa Barbara:

> *As we drew near, we heard the accustomed sound of violins and guitars, and saw a great motion of the people within. Going in, we found nearly all the people of the town—men, women, and children—collected and crowded in the room, leaving barely room for the dancers, for on these occasions no invitations are given, but everyone is expected to come, though there is always a private entertainment within the house for particular friends.*

A ranching family celebrates in front of their home, playing musical instruments and dancing a traditional Spanish dance called the fandango. The women wear colorful dresses for a special occasion and the men wear short, embroidered jackets with leather chaps (trousers) and cummerbunds (wide belts).

Dana also observed another unusual custom at the wedding celebration: "*The great amusement of the evening—owing to its being the Carnival—was the breaking of eggs, filled with cologne or other essences, upon the heads of the company. The women bring a great number of these secretly about them, and the amusement is to break one upon the head of a gentleman when his back is turned.*"

Other entertainments at weddings included displays of bullfighting, cockfighting, fights between bears, bulls, and dogs, and horsemanship. Before a cockfight, one visitor to California was shocked to see the small spurs attached to the legs of the birds.

The rancheros had neither time for nor interest in formal education. Book learning was valued less than the ability to run a ranch properly, and literacy was rare. Public schools were not supported by the Mexican government, and in 1834, there were only three public primary schools in California.

New Mexican Citizens

Not all the wealthy ranchers in California were of Spanish or Mexican origin. Some Americans, recognizing an opportunity to get their hands on large parcels of land, decided to convert to Catholicism and become naturalized Mexican citizens. As citizens of Mexico, they, too, were given huge plots of land for ranching.

One man who became a Mexican citizen was John Marsh. Marsh, fleeing from bill collectors and the law, arrived in California in 1836. Although he didn't have a degree in medicine, Marsh used his Harvard diploma to obtain a doctor's license from the Los Angeles *ayuntamiento.* California's first practicing "doctor" accepted cash, cattle, and hides as payment. In 1837, Marsh converted to Catholicism, became a Mexican citizen, and was allowed to purchase a ranch in present-day Contra Costa County.

Marsh actively encouraged his friends in Massachusetts to migrate to California. He disapproved of the way Mexico governed its northern colony and believed that, with enough settlers, Americans could take control. In November 1835, Americans in Texas had done just that, forming their own government and battling and winning independence from Mexico.

Marsh was well aware that Mexico had few soldiers in California. Those who were there were poorly armed. Marsh and others who visited or settled in California during the Mexican period could easily predict what the future held in store. Englishman George Simpson wrote, *"The Americans, if masters of the interior, will soon discover that they have a natural right to a maritime outlet, so that, whatever may be the fate of Monterey and the more southerly ports, San Francisco will . . . sooner or later fall into the hands of the Americans."*

CHAPTER EIGHT

The Americans Take Over

MEXICO AND THE UNITED STATES *go to war, and Americans in California take the opportunity to seize control.*

On October 19, 1842, Californios in Monterey were shocked to look out their windows and find that they had been invaded by U.S. troops. A group of marines, led by Commodore Thomas Catesby Jones, commander of the U.S. Navy's Pacific Fleet, was patrolling the waters off the coast of California. Mistakenly hearing that the United States and Mexico were at war, Jones had seized the opportunity to attack.

OPPOSITE: During the Siege of Monterey, U.S. soldiers fought the Mexican Army in hand-to-hand combat in the streets as well as in the harbor and in the mountains above the city. The chaos of the third day of battle is depicted in this hand-colored, 1846 lithograph.

When he was informed that he was wrong by an American merchant living in Monterey, Jones apologized and quickly left.

Unhappy Californians

American settlers in California disliked being controlled by Mexican officials. California's last Mexican governor, Manuel Micheltorena, sent to California in 1842, had problems from the start. The Californios immediately resented him, and he couldn't control his Mexican soldiers, many of whom were recruited straight from Mexican jails. In 1845, a number of important landowners rose up against him. Although no one was injured during an exchange of gunfire, Micheltorena was thrown out of the colony. The landowners replaced him with Pio Pico, a landowner from San Diego. Pico, born at Mission San Gabriel in 1801, was a lifelong California resident. He was the first multicultural governor, since he was of Spanish, African, and Native American descent. As governor, Pico moved the capital of California to Los Angeles.

Pio Pico was the Spanish governor of California from 1845 to 1846, the year the United States took California from Mexico.

By 1845, about a thousand Americans had settled in California. Many of these Americans were squatters, illegally making their homes in unpopulated areas. Unwilling to convert to Catholicism or become Mexican citizens, the new arrivals were unable to gain legal title from Mexico to the land they were living on. They constantly feared being evicted from their new homes.

squatter—a person who settles illegally on land owned by someone else

Governor Pico was unhappy about the increased number of American settlers coming into the region. In the summer of 1845, he issued a command telling Californios to get ready to defend their land from a U.S. invasion.

Around this time, the phrase "manifest destiny" was gaining popularity in the United States. Created by an American magazine editor, the term referred to the growing belief that Americans were entitled to rule the entire North American continent. In California, most American settlers heartily agreed. In 1846, newly arrived settler Edwin Bryant described the scene at a San Francisco dinner party. "*It was very difficult for me to realize that I was many thousand miles from home, in a strange and foreign country,*" he wrote. "*All the faces about me were American . . . . Indeed, it seems to be a settled opinion, that California is henceforth to compose a part of the United States, and every American who is now here considers himself as treading upon his own soil, as much as if he were in one of the old thirteen revolutionary states.*"

The Bear Flag Revolt

John Frémont, leader of the Bear Flag revolt

In December 1845, John Charles Frémont and 60 armed men arrived in California. An army captain, Frémont told California officials that he and his men had been sent there by the U.S. Army to map wagon passes through the Sierras. California's military commander, José Castro, didn't believe Frémont and ordered him out of the territory in March 1846. Castro correctly guessed that the American officer was there spying and encouraging American settlers to revolt against Mexican rule.

Frémont's banishment fueled rumors that American squatters would also soon be evicted. The American settlers now prepared for action. On June 14, 1846, about 90 armed settlers in Sonoma revolted against Mexican rule.

The rebels easily took control of Sonoma, Mexico's headquarters in northern California. They captured the town's mayor along with General Mariano Vallejo, one of the richest and most important men in California, and locked them up in Sutter's Fort. The rebels fashioned a flag with a bear on it and raised the banner over Sonoma. As a result, their new "country" was known as the Bear Flag Republic of Independent California.

Frémont arrived in Sonoma several days after the rebels had taken control. He aided the Americans until July, when word came that the United States and Mexico were at war and that Monterey had been invaded by U.S. forces. At this point, the Bear Flag Republic was dissolved, and the fight for the entire California territory began.

The flag of the Bear Flag Republic was raised over Sonoma on June 14, 1846. It represented the American victory over the Mexican rulers of northern California.

THE MEXICAN-AMERICAN WAR

When planning their revolt in late May, American settlers in Sonoma had no way of knowing that the United States was already at war with Mexico. Tensions between the two neighboring nations had been simmering since

December 1845, when the United States annexed Texas, formerly owned by Mexico. At that time, Mexico broke off diplomatic relations with the United States, and the two countries began bickering about the exact location of the Texas-Mexico border.

On April 24, 1846, Mexican soldiers crossed the Rio Grande into land claimed by both the United States and Mexico and attacked U.S. troops. On May 13, 1846, the United States officially declared war on Mexico. By July, U.S. troops under General Stephen W. Kearny had captured the Mexican territory of New Mexico. The following month, Kearny and his men set out to conquer California.

The first armed forces had already arrived in California not by land, but by sea. On July 7, 1846, U.S. Navy commander John D. Sloat raised the U.S. flag in Monterey. He announced that *"henceforward, California will be a portion of the United States."*

In August, Navy officer Robert F. Stockton marched into Los Angeles, where he learned that Pio Pico, José Castro, and the Mexican troops had evacuated the town and moved south. Stockton declared himself military governor of California and issued a statement in which he promised to be fair to all residents. It read, *"All persons, of whatever religion or nation, who faithfully adhere to the new government, will be considered as citizens of the Territory, and will be zealously and thoroughly protected in their liberty of conscience, their persons, and property."*

Californio Resistance

The Mexican War divided Californios and tested their loyalties. Some accepted the U.S. takeover and tried to cooperate with the new rulers. They hoped that getting along with the Americans would enable them to obtain a good job or some property to manage. This attitude often earned them the contempt of their family and friends. San Diego merchant Miguel de Pedrorena supported the American takeover. He wrote to an American friend, "*I find my friend Aguirre so much like a lamb in my presence is taking every opportunity of speaking against me and wounding my feelings in every possible way and manner. I hope that he and I will meet again and if there is not hot water enough to scald one of us it is a pity I forgave him once on account of Family relationship but that will not avail him again.*"

Many Californios, however, resented the American invaders. Some tried to resist the occupation and take back their land. The high point of Californio resistance occurred outside San Diego on December 6, 1846, when 93 Californios attacked a detachment of U.S. soldiers under General Kearny. At the Battle of San Pasqual, the Californios nearly wiped out Kearny's troops. Luckily for the commander, reinforcements from San Diego arrived late in the day and allowed the Americans to retreat safely. In all, 19 Americans and 6 Californios were killed, with many more on both sides wounded.

California's Native Americans tried to remain neutral but were pulled into the conflict. One man who was both Californio and Indian related a visit with a Mexican soldier before the Battle of San Pasqual: "*My father, Pontho the chief, was brave, so he went to talk with the soldiers; their head man was called General Pico, and to him my father spoke. This man said we might come and live in the huts the soldiers did not need, so at night we crept back, for it was cold, and the rain was falling. There were few houses left for so many, and little food, but we said nothing.*" The Indians were also pressed into service for both sides.

Some Indians took the chance to strike back at the Spanish and Mexicans who had oppressed them for so long. During the war, some Indians raided nearby ranchos. One of the bloodiest incidents of retaliation, called the Pauma Massacre, took place soon after the Battle of San Pasqual. A group of Luiseño Indians captured 11 Californio men and youths and killed them with spears. The Californios retaliated by sending out a force that killed more than a hundred of the Luiseño. Twenty more were taken captive and later executed.

Although the Californios put up a fight for their land, Governor Pico knew that they would be unable to withstand the superior forces of the U.S. military for much longer. In August 1846, he fled to Mexico, and on January 13, 1847, Mexican Army captain José María Flores and Andres Pico, the governor's brother, surrendered to American troops. The United States had taken California.

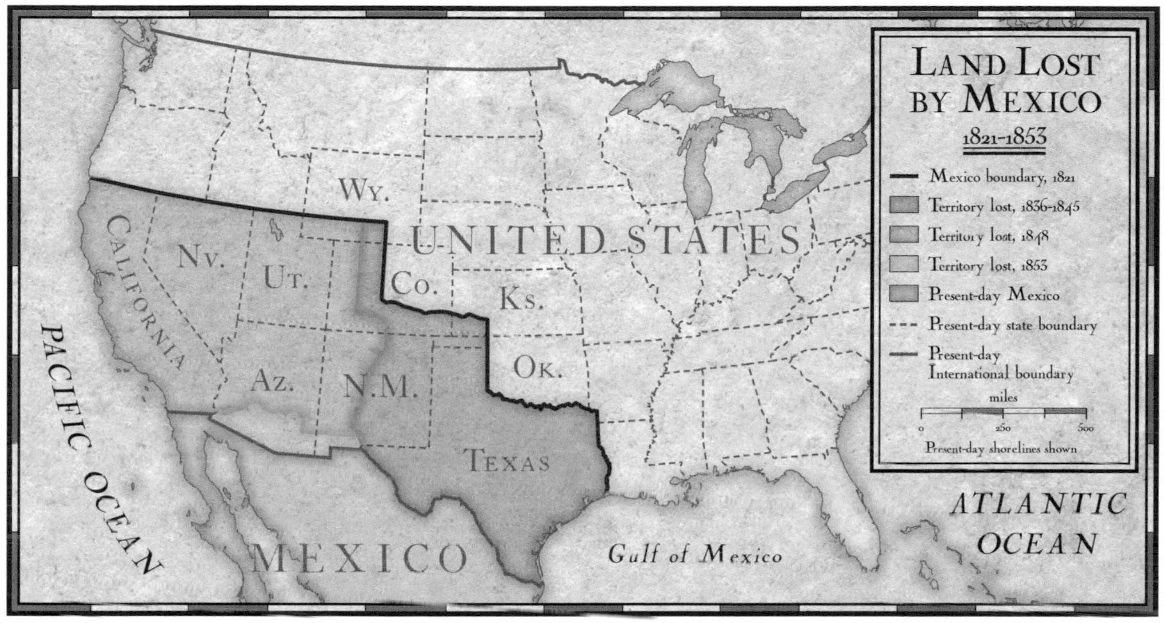

The red line on this map shows how far north and east the boundary of Mexico stretched in 1821 when it won its independence from Spain. Between 1836 and 1853, Mexico lost the land that now makes up all or part of ten present-day U.S. states (green areas). The influence of this Hispanic heritage is still strong throughout this region.

THE WAR ENDS

In early 1848, the Mexican-American War came to an end. On February 2, the two countries signed the Treaty of Guadalupe Hidalgo. Under the terms of the treaty, Mexico ceded about half its territory—including California—to the United States.

In September 1849, a group of 48 delegates gathered at Monterey and drew up a constitution. The constitution, modeled after New York's, banned slavery. Two months later, the document was passed by popular vote, and California's civil government went into effect.

Californios quickly found themselves stripped of their social, political, and financial power. But what the Americans wanted most from the Californios was the thousands of acres of land they controlled. American officials now hauled wealthy rancheros into court, forcing them to prove their claim to the land they owned. Forced to pay high fees to English-speaking attorneys, the once-wealthy Californios now found themselves selling their ranchos to American settlers to pay off their debts. Many Californios would lose everything they had.

The Gold Rush Begins

On January 24, 1848, gold was discovered on the American River at Sutter's Mill near Sacramento. James Marshall, John Sutter's partner, explained, "*My eye was caught by something shining in the bottom of the ditch. . . . I reached my hand down and picked it up; it made my heart thump, for I was certain it was gold. . . . Then I saw another.*"

Over the next two years, more than 85,000 people arrived in California in the hopes of striking it rich. People came from all over the world. Ships lay abandoned in San Francisco harbor as their crews deserted to head for California's goldfields. In ten years' time, the number of non-native people in California skyrocketed to around 380,000.

The Sierra Nevada, mountains in northern California, were flooded with propsectors and miners after gold fever hit the nation.

Gold fever was often just that — a sickness that caused all kinds of bad behavior. At Mission San Fernando Rey, rumors of buried gold caused seekers to knock down the mission's walls and dig up the floors in order to find the "padre's gold."

The gold rush boosted San Francisco's growth. After the war, the tiny town had developed slowly. But now growth accelerated rapidly. San Francisco became a thriving port where would-be millionaires arrived, stayed, and spent their money. New houses, hotels, and shops sprang up almost overnight.

PROFILE

James Wilson Marshall

Born in New Jersey in 1810, James Wilson Marshall emigrated to California in 1845. Marshall worked as a carpenter there and bought some land near Sutter's Fort. A year later, he took part in the Bear Flag Revolt and fought in the Mexican-American War.

In 1847, Marshall teamed up with John Sutter to build and run a sawmill on the American River. On January 24, 1848, Marshall was checking the sawmill to make sure it was running properly. As he looked into the water, he saw several small flakes of gold. At this time, California was still officially a Mexican territory. No treaties between Mexico and the United States had yet been signed.

Although Marshall was the first person to find gold in California, he didn't benefit from his discovery. None of his claims were ever recognized as valid. At the age of 75, he died a poor man. Today, visitors to Marshall Gold Discovery State Historic Park, in Coloma, can see a replica of Marshall's original sawmill as well as gold rush artifacts.

Many people who came to California during the gold rush wanted the gold-rich territory to become a U.S. state. As early as July 1848, citizens were being encouraged by U.S. military officials to press for statehood. The boom in population and business—thanks to the gold rush—had proved that California was capable of being a self-supporting state.

On September 9, 1850, California became the 31st U.S. state. It was allowed into the Union under the Compromise of 1850. Under the terms of this legislation, California was admitted as a free state, meaning slavery was not allowed, but the nation adopted stricter laws to capture and return runaway slaves to appease the southern states. Sacramento, an important gold rush town, was named the capital. California had grown slowly under Spanish, then Mexican control. Now, as part of the United States, its greatest growth was still ahead.

California's gold had an immediate impact, not only on the state itself, but on the nation as a whole. For example, gold from California helped to finance the Union cause during the Civil War (1861–1865). Even when gold mining declined after 1852, the new state's favorable climate and fertile land continued to lure more and more people out West. Today, California is not only the most populous U.S. state, but also one of the most economically successful. It has come a long way since the days when both Spanish missionaries and Native Indians struggled for survival. ※

Time Line

1492 Spain begins its conquest of the New World when Christopher Columbus claims several Caribbean islands.

1535 Hernán Cortés, conqueror of Aztec Mexico, founds a Spanish settlement on the peninsula known today as Baja (Lower) California.

1542 Portuguese-born explorer Juan Rodríguez Cabrillo becomes the first European to explore the coast of present-day California.

1579 English pirate Sir Francis Drake sails to California and claims the area for England.

1602 Sebastián Vizcaíno sails from Acapulco, Mexico, to present-day San Diego, naming many places along the way.

1769 Prompted by foreign exploration of the region, New Spain sends out a "sacred expedition" to found missions and presidios in California; on July 16, Junípero Serra founds Mission San Diego de Alcalá, the first Spanish settlement in California.

1770 Mission San Carlos Borromeo de Monterey is founded.

1774 Juan Bautista de Anza forges an overland route from New Spain to California.

1775 Kumeyaay Indians living near Mission San Diego rise up in revolt against the Spanish missionaries.

1776 Anza selects a site near San Francisco Bay for a new mission and presidio.

1792 English explorer George Vancouver visits San Francisco Bay.

1806 Russian trade official Nikolai Petrovich Rezanov arrives in San Francisco to establish a trade link between Russia's Alaskan trading posts and Spain's California settlements.

1810 Mexico begins fighting for independence from Spain.

1812 The Russian-American Company founds a trading post at Fort Ross.

1818 French pirate Hippolyte Bouchard burns parts of Monterey and Mission San Juan Capistrano.

1821 Mexico wins its independence from Spain.

1825 The first Mexican governor, José María Echeandía, arrives in California.

1826 Jedediah Strong Smith arrives at Mission San Gabriel, becoming the first American to reach California from the east by land.

1833 California governor Jose Luís Figueroa begins the process of turning the territory's 21 missions into ranchos.

1835 The tiny trading post of Yerba Buena is founded; in the coming years, the town will grow and be renamed San Francisco.

1840 Richard Henry Dana's book *Two Years Before the Mast* encourages many Americans to migrate to California.

1841 The first organized group of American settlers, the Bidwell-Bartelson party, arrives in California.

1842 American Navy officer Thomas Catesby Jones, mistakenly believing that the United States and Mexico are at war, captures the town of Monterey.

1846 The United States declares war on Mexico.

1846 In June, American settlers take control of Sonoma during the Bear Flag Revolt and declare the area an independent republic; in July, American troops take control of Monterey and, soon after, Yerba Buena, San Diego, Santa Barbara, and Los Angeles; in December, Californios triumph over the American invaders in the Battle of San Pasqual.

1847 In January, California officials surrender to American troops.

1848 In January, gold is found at Sutter's Mill; in February, the Mexican-American War ends; California is ceded to the United States.

1850 On September 9, California becomes the 31st U.S. state.

Resources

BOOKS

Keremitsis, Eileen. *Life in a California Mission.* San Diego: Lucent Books, 2002.

Paddison, Joshua. *A World Transformed: Firsthand Accounts of California Before the Gold Rush.* Berkeley, Calif.: Heyday Books, 1999.

Porterfield, Jason. *The Treaty of Guadalupe Hidalgo, 1848: A Primary Source Examination of the Treaty That Ended the Mexican-American War.* New York: Rosen Central, 2005.

Whiting, Jim. *Gaspar de Portolá.* Hockessin, Del.: Mitchell Lane Publishers, 2002.

———. *Junípero Jose Serra.* Hockessin, Del.: Mitchell Lane Publishers, 2003.

Williams, Jack S. *Soldiers and Their Families of the California Mission Frontier.* New York: Rosen Publishing Group, 2003.

WEB SITES

California History Online
http://www.learncalifornia.org
An electronic resource for people interested in California history from the Secretary of State

California Missions Resource Center
http://www.missionscalifornia.com
A guide to California's historic missions

Early California History
http://lcweb2.loc.gov/ammem/cbhtml/cbintro.html A history of early California from the Library of Congress

Mexican Museum
http://www.mexicanmuseum.org
Home page of San Francisco's Mexican Museum

New Perspectives on the West
http://www.pbs.org/weta/thewest/intro.htm
A Web site featuring the history of the West, including information on the people and events that shaped California's history

Quote Sources

CHAPTER ONE

p.14 "completely populated…among them." Bouvier, Virginia Marie. *Women and the Conquest of California, 1542–1840.* Tuscon, AZ: The University of Arizona Press, 2001, p. 6; p. 15 "gave…fear." Gutiérrez, Ramón A. and Richard J. Orsi (editors.) *Contested Eden: California Before the Gold Rush.* Berkeley: University of California Press, 1998, p. 85; "bearded…armed" Gutiérrez, p. 15; p. 19 "without…could enter." Landberg, Leif C. W. *The Chumash Indians of Southern California.* Los Angeles: Southland Press, Inc., 1956, p. 26.

CHAPTER TWO

p. 27 "less…Mary." Brown, Alan K. (editor). *A Description of Distant Roads: Original Journals of the First Expedition into California, 1769–1770.* San Diego: San Diego State University Press, 2001, p. 317; p. 28 "When they…anywhere here." Brown, p. 553; "When the…his friend." Gutiérrez, Ramón A. and Richard J. Orsi (editors.) *Contested Eden: California Before the Gold Rush.* Berkeley: University of California Press, 1998, pp. 69–70.

CHAPTER THREE

p. 34 "train them up…civilised society." Heizer, Robert F. and Alan F. Almquist. *The Other Californians: Prejudice and Discrimination Under Spain, Mexico, and the United States to 1920.* Berkeley, CA: University of California Press, 1971, p. 5; p. 35 "The padres…taken." Bouvier, Virginia Marie. *Women and the Conquest of California, 1542–1840.* Tuscon, AZ: The University of Arizona Press, 2001, p. 91; p. 35 http://www.missionscalifornia.com; "…any of their forefathers." Heizer, pp. 5–6; p. 37 "are ignorant…Mission Bell." http://www.missionscalifornia.com; p. 38 "with whips…fixed bayonets." Paddison, Joshua (editor). *A World Transformed: Firsthand Accounts of California Before the Gold Rush.* Berkeley, CA: Heyday Books, 1999, p. 192; p. 41 "They are…of mice." Bolton, Herbert Eugene. *Outpost of Empire: The Story of the Founding of San Francisco.* New York: A.A. Knopf, 1931, p.3; "I might inquire…everything." Heizer and Almquist, p. 3; p. 42 "I confess…to my country." http://www.missionscalifornia.com; "There are…the Lord." http://www.missionscalifornia.com, "The Indians…treacherous disposition." Heizer, p. 4; pp. 42–43 "The treatment…without water." Riesenberg, Felix Jr. *The Golden Road.* New York: McGraw-Hill Book Company, Inc., 1962, p. 50; p. 45 "[The runaway]…the others." Paddison, p. 118.

CHAPTER FOUR

pp. 48–49 "The floor…of the globe." Paddison, Joshua (editor). *A World Transformed: Firsthand Accounts of California Before the Gold Rush.* Berkeley, CA: Heyday Books, 1999, pp. 73–74; "There is…civilized nation." Paddison, p. 76; pp. 49–50 "Little…the [Indian] women." http://www.sandiegohistory.org.

CHAPTER FIVE

p. 58 "I was…careless indifference." Paddison, Joshua (editor). *A World Transformed: Firsthand Accounts of California Before the Gold Rush.* Berkeley, CA: Heyday Books, 1999, p. 80; p. 60 "Thereupon I…military defenses." Paddison, p. 104; "barren island…a trace." Paddison, p. 105; p. 61 "The bright…Nueva California." Paddison, p. 122; "a beautiful…nothing else." Paddison, p. 122; pp. 63–64 "The misery…seeing bread." Paddison, pp. 141–142; p. 64 "Necessity…by law." Gutiérrez, Ramón A. and Richard J. Orsi (editors.) *Contested Eden: California Before the Gold Rush.* Berkeley: University of California Press, 1998, p. 129.

CHAPTER SIX

pp. 72–73 "The natives…slave labor." Hastings, Lansford Warren. *The Emigrants' Guide to Oregon and California.* Facsimile produced in Ann Arbor, MI: University Microfilms, 1968, p. 132; pp. 72–73 "The troops…the back." http://www.cr.nps.gov; p. 73 "I passed…his sorrow." Bryant, Edwin. *What I Saw in California.* Ebook@http://www.gutenberg.org; p. 74 "A country…economy." Ebook@http://www.gutenberg.org; p. 76 "blessed with…the world." Dana, Richard Henry Jr. *Two Years Before the Mast.* Boston: Houghton Mifflin Company, 1911, p. 216; "In the…might be!" Dana, p. 216; p. 78 "O Mary…as you can." Werner, Emmy E. *Pioneer Children on the Journey West.* Boulder, CO: Westview Press, 1995, p. 8; p. 79 "Where my…absent husband." Holmes, Kenneth L. *Covered Wagon Women: Diaries & Letters from the Western Trails, 1840–1849, Volume I.* Lincoln, NE: University of Nebraska Press, 1995, p. 81.

CHAPTER SEVEN

p. 82 "The Indians…for the women." Dana, Richard Henry Jr. *Two Years Before the Mast.* Boston: Houghton Mifflin Company, 1911, p. 100; p. 83 "A gentleman…without difficulty." Bryant, Edwin. *What I Saw in California.* Ebook@http://www.gutenberg.org; p. 84 "The fondness…and necklace." Dana, p. 96; p. 85 "The little…importance." Bryant, Ebook; p. 86 "The houses…on the outside." Dana, p. 100; p. 87 "As we drew…particular friends." Dana, p. 302; p. 88 "The great…is turned." Dana, p. 215; p. 89 "The Americans…of the Americans." Owens, Kenneth N. *John Sutter and a Wider West.* Omaha, NE: University of Nebraska Press, p. 36.

CHAPTER EIGHT

p. 93 "It was…revolutionary states." Bryant, Edwin. *What I Saw in California.* Ebook@http://www.gutenberg.org; p. 96 "henceforward…United States." Gutiérrez, Ramón A. and Richard J. Orsi (editors.) *Contested Eden: California Before the Gold Rush.* Berkeley: University of California Press, 1998, p. 338; p. 97 "I find…him again." http://www.sandiegohistory.org; p. 98 "My father,…said nothing." http://www.sandiegohistory.org; p. 100 "My eye…another." http://lcweb2.loc.gov.

INDEX

About the Author and Consultant

ROBIN DOAK is a writer of fiction and nonfiction books for children, ranging from elementary to high school levels. Subjects she has written about include American immigration, the 50 states, American presidents, and U.S. geography. Doak is a former editor of *Weekly Reader* and has also written numerous support guides for educators. She holds a Bachelor of Arts degree in English, with an emphasis on journalism, from the University of Connecticut and lives near her alma mater in Portland. Doak is also the author of *Voices from Colonial America: New Jersey*.

ANDRÉS RESÉNDEZ is an associate professor of history at the University of California at Davis. He earned his Ph.D. in history from the University of Chicago. A native of Mexico, Reséndez has written numerous books and articles on the history of the American Southwest. He is also the consultant for *Voices from Colonial America: Texas* and resides in Davis, California.

Illustration Credits

Cover : Courtesy of University of Southern California, on behalf of the USC Specialized Libraries and Archival Collections.

End sheets, pages 15, 82, 90: The Library of Congress

Title page, pages 9, 31, 32, 43, 45, 72, 77, 80, 84, 94, 102: Courtesy of The Bancroft Library, University of California, Berkeley

Pages 8 (inset), 75, 99: National Geographic

Pages 11, 12, 22, 27, 53, 58, 65, 68, 87, 95: The Granger Collection

Page 17: Picture Collection, The Branch Libraries, The New York Public Library, Astor, Lenox and Tilden Foundation

Pages 19, 48, 101: Art Resource

Pages 35, 36, 38, 92: North Wind Picture Archives

Pages 46, 56: California Historical Society

Pages 61, 62: Courtesy of Santa Clara Historic Archives/ Warburton Collection

Page 85: Bridgeman Art Library

NORTH AMERICA Divided into its III PRINCIPALL PARTS 1st ENGLISH Part Viz ENGLISH EMPIRE
N Foundland N Scotland N England N York N Jarsey Pensylvania Maryland Virginia Carolina Carolania or Florida California, Sommer Is Bahama Is Jamaica & ye CARIBY Is II SPANISH
1685
BAFFI BAY
ARCTI
NEW NORTH WALES
NEW SOUTH WALES
Tract of Land full of Wild Bulls
NEW MEXICO
New Mexico
NEW ALBION
CALIFORNIA
SEA OF CALIFORNIA
NEW BISCAIA
ZACATECAS
THE GOLF OR BAY OF MEXICO
LAKE SUPERIOR
LAKE HURONS
SEA OF NEW SPAIN
YUCATAN
HONDURAS